IN LIVING MEMORY

LIFE IN 'THE BOROUGHS'

The Boroughs and Horsemarket Living Memory Project

Louise Amos, Margaret Andrews, Sue Bell, Julia Bush, Angela Connor
Linn Dhaidan, Jim and Pat Edwards, Richard Foreman
Diana Lyon, Greta Matthews, John and Edna Short, Bob Stanton
Jon Small, Kate Wills

———ooOoo———

A Northampton Arts Development Publication

Spencer-Dallington Community Centre
Tintern Avenue
Northampton NN5 7BZ

'Phone (0604) 583539

First published in 1987 by Northampton Arts Development, Spencer-Dallington Community Centre, Tintern Avenue, Northampton NN5 7BZ. Tel: (0604) 583539

ISBN 0-9512329-0-8

Acknowlegements

For individual help:
Christine Ablett, Dominic Allard, Marie Barnard, Alan Burman, Chris Casey, Heather Collins, Rick Cook, Bill Coulson, Marie Dickie, George Freeston, Lionel Gent, Bill and Carol Going, Frank Green, Judith Hodgkinson, Ron Johnson, Neville Kirby, Roger Kitchen, Ruth Lambert, Ruth Lewis, Maria Limonci, Rosemary McCarlie, Terry McClure, Cleve McCollin, Lily O'Halloran, Tom Paintain, Louis Peters, John Rawlings, Stephanie Record, June Swann, Mr. & Mrs. Thornton, Louise Turner, Rachel Watson, Alan Williams and to all interviewees and contributors of written material.

Organisations:

Northampton Borough Council (especially Housing, Public Relations and Leisure and Recreation departments), Northampton Central Library (and Duston and Weston Favell branches), Northamptonshire Police, Northampton Museums, Northampton Social Services, Boys and Girls Brigade, Doddridge and Commercial Street United Reformed Church, South Midlands Co-operative Society, Spring Lane School, Chronicle and Echo, Radio Northampton, Northants '96.

For financial help:

East Midlands Arts, Northampton Borough Council, Hammon Osborne, Barclaycard, Alan Moore.

Typesetting by Optical Character Recognition, Room 16, Whitworth Chambers, George Row, Northampton.

Printed by T. Clarke (Printing) Ltd., Northampton

In respectful memory: Ron George – 1917–1987.

CONTENTS

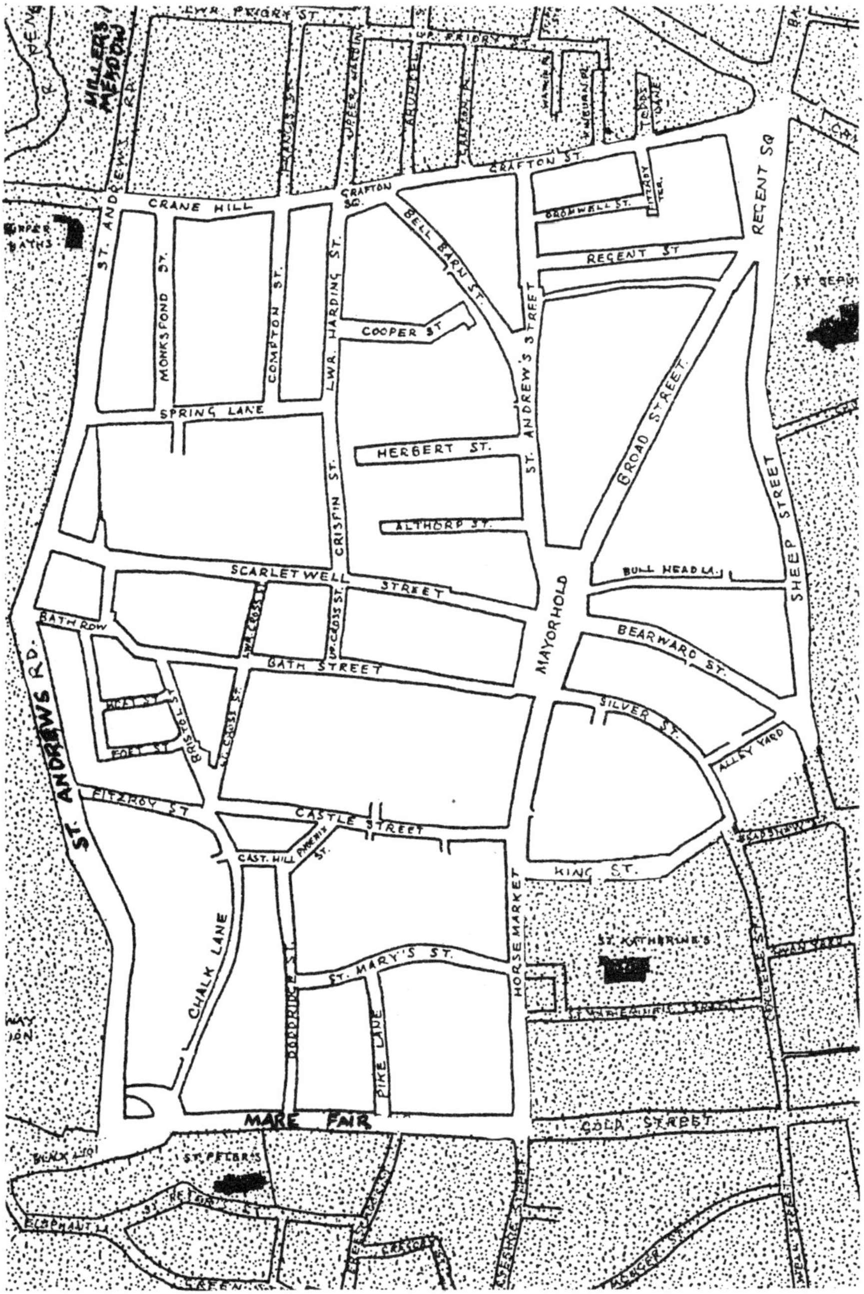
LWR PRIORY ST
UP. PRIORY ST
MILLERS MEADOW
ST. ANDREWS RD.
GRAFTON ST.
REGENT SQ
CRANE HILL
GRAFTON SQ.
BELL BARN ST.
CROMWELL ST.
FITZROY TER.
REGENT ST
MONKSFOND ST.
COMPTON ST.
LWR. HARDING ST.
COOPER ST
SPRING LANE
ST. ANDREW'S STREET
BROAD STREET
SHEEP STREET
HERBERT ST.
ALTHORP ST.
CRISPIN ST.
SCARLETWELL STREET
BULL HEAD LA.
BATH ROW
MAYORHOLD
BEARWARD ST.
BATH STREET
SILVER ST.
BRISTOL ST
ALLEY YARD
FITZROY ST
CASTLE STREET
CAST. HILL
PHOENIX ST.
KING ST.
CHALK LANE
HORSEMARKET
ST. KATHERINE'S
ST. MARY'S ST.
PIKE LANE
MARE FAIR
GOLD STREET
ST. PETER'S
HORSESHOE STREET

PREFACE

Most of the words in this book have been spoken or written by people who were born, or have lived in the 'Boroughs' area of Northampton.

Conversations, by their nature, tend to drift from one subject to another and back again. Most of us, when we speak, tend to repeat ourselves. Many of us frequently repeat words such as 'you know' or 'like'. Sometimes we don't bother to complete the sentence we're saying when it's obvious the person we're speaking to knows what we mean.

To make tape-recorded conversations readable and relevant, on paper, we have had to edit the material. We have cut out words, phrases and some of the questions we asked. Sometimes we've changed the order in which the words were spoken. Sometimes we've had to fill in gaps with words of our own. Whenever we've done this, we've put the words we've added in brackets (). Our intention, in doing this, is not to distort or change the meaning of anything we've been told, but to try and make it clearer to the reader. If, we have made any mistakes in doing this, we apologise to the speakers concerned and will attempt to rectify them in any future editions of this book.

Material has been arranged into chapters on different aspects of life in the area. Decisions as to which piece should go in which chapter were not always easy to make and there were times when to cut up and divide the words people wrote or spoke seemed a shame. So you will not find all the material in this book fits easily into the chapters. A few pieces have been left to stand outside them.

We hope you find this book interesting and enjoyable to read. It's not intended to be an authoritative history of the area. It's a collection of memories, and no one will agree with all of them exactly. We hope this book will serve as a tribute to and a record of a community that once existed in the 'good old town' of Northampton.

Aerial Photograph courtesy Northampton Independent, 1920.

NO ARTIFICIAL ADDITIVES

Cottage Delight Ltd
Speciality Foods.

CEE
64 11 B
PRODUCE OF FRANCE

FAB
1058

WILD BOAR PATE
WITH COGNAC

REFRIGERATE AFTER OPENING
THEN CONSUME WITHIN 3 DAYS

ingredients: wild boar, pork (lean, fat & liver), cognac (1%), salt, pepper, spices.

MINIMUM 95% MEAT

NET WT.
190g 6·7oz

station road. cheddleton. leek. staffs. 0538 361011

INTRODUCTION

Why it was called 'Boroughs' I'll never know. I would imagine it may have had something to do with so many villains like rats scuffling about in burrows... I've often asked. The first thing the sergeant told you when he sent you – "You're down the Boroughs tonight, boy," "What do you call it the Boroughs for, sergeant?" "Get on you, don't ask silly questions." He didn't know!

(Ex-Detective Chief Inspector George Harding)

The reason the area was called the Burrows was because so many houses, shops and public houses were built so tightly close to each other in such a small area of the Borough Town Centre. Also, in the same area was the Borough's main Refuse Depot where the town's rubbish was collected and burnt in large furnaces causing plenty of black smoke. This meant continuous hard work in many ways for the people living in the area to keep everything clean. There were no such things as mechanical (cleaning) devices at this time of the century. There was also a power station close to.

(Reg Caiger)

John Stevens: I've always been a little bit intrigued by this name 'The Boroughs'. Some people think it was because they bred rather rapidly like rabbits, but I don't think that's true. This business of large families was just as true of every other part of every other town because in that time there was no such thing as family planning. I think it's to do with the original Borough. I've got a map, 1720 odd, which shows the area of the town. Just about the area we're talking of.

Kate Wills: Of course, it was within the old town wall.

John Stevens: I'm sure that's where the name really came from. The fact that they've associated it with rabbits – it's a thing the better-off have thought of.

The Borough Yard ran along Little Cross Street, along the bottom with the old, big destructor chimney. A terrific chimney. But that's why, in my opinion, we got the name: 'The Borough Boys'. It was nothing to do with living in rabbit burrows. I think we got it from the fact that the Borough Yard was in Bath Street. So they called us: 'The Borough Boys' who lived in the vicinity of the Borough Yard, which I say now is Scarletwell Street, Castle Street, Bath Street, any little intersecting streets and the Mayorhold. That was the Boroughs, what we called the Boroughs.

(Reg Tero)

It was just happiness, wasn't it? Wasn't a lot of money but there was friendship and happiness. No greedy people, if you know what I mean. If you didn't have a crust and they'd got one, they'd break it in half and give it to you. That's the sort of people they were. They were rough and ready, but very, very kind, deep down.

(Mrs Eileen Allard)

Everyone seemed to know each other. You'd all help each other out... And we lived near the town you see. Used to cut through. We was younger those days... it didn't seem half so far. But round here it was all pubs. Every street there was a pub each end. It's a marvel how people done the trade.

(Mrs Elizabeth Whitney)

It was the poorest part of the town, then. But they were good people, gooder than what they are today. They don't keep up with the Joneses back in them days like they do today. Half of them didn't have a hot meal them days. My mother's given a few a meal. They'd help you. Not like today – run past your door.

Of course (you) wouldn't dream about locking your door. Unless you went out – you might lock it then. But at night time you wouldn't have to dream of locking it. There weren't such things going on, them days.

(Dennis Verrechia).

The things that used to happen then, they seem almost unbelievable today. Nobody ever locked their doors when they went out, quite often left them ajar and it was nothing unusual for people to go wandering in other people's houses. That was the sort of thing they were. All friends and petty rivalries, I suppose, disagreements and a bit of shouting over the back wall and that sort of thing. But on the whole it was a real community.

(Cyril Benton)

People lived rough in those days, but they lived better lives, I'm sure. There are people who say that people lived because of fear of hell-fire and that sort of thing. I think that's rubbish. I think that people respected each other. We lived in Crispin Street, and my mother had gone into town and left the door open for us children, to come home from school, to get in the house. You couldn't do that today.

(John Stevens).

Julia Bush: Do you miss the sense of community that used to be in the Boroughs?

Josephine Kent: Oh yes. I can remember, when we were little, there were people always having babies, and they used to say: "Oh, Alice Walding I'll look after her – she's having a baby." I can remember different children being in our house, 'cause our mother looked after them – just 'til the actual birth was over.

You'd never see anybody without a meal. I mean, there wasn't an awful lot but there was that friendship among people. They wouldn't see one another without a meal. You don't see that today.

Irene Swainsbury: If anybody was in trouble there was always somebody to help. I don't mean trouble in wrong doing but, say somebody had been taken ill or something, there was always somebody ready to go and help.

It was quite normal for one to go out and leave one's doors unlocked. Any trouble developing, various neighbours would come in to see what they could do for you. It was a very strong community. (For example) my mother slipped on the ice one Christmas Day and hurt her thigh very badly. It was soon over the neighbourhood and I can remember on the Monday morning when Dad had to go to work, of course, there were several ladies came in to see what they could do. See what chores they could perform. No one ever thought of any payment. It was all done purely out of neighbourliness.

(Bill Coulson).

Peggy Ward: I remember people sitting outside their houses. The women would all be on their doorsteps when I went to school there. I remember going home and telling my mother about it.

Miss V. Godfrey: They were such poor houses, it was better for them to sit outside.

(Peggy Ward and Miss V. Godfrey were teachers at Spring Lane School. Miss Ward was also a pupil there).

Lucy Starmer: Everybody helped everybody. I suppose everybody told you that. If a child was being born, all the kids were pushed into another house out of the way, until it was all over. And take the mother a cup of tea, you know.

Kate Wills: There was a 'community'.

Richard Foreman: I get the impression that people were pretty poor in the area.

Lucy Starmer: Well, you know, there's some made more of what little they had than others you see. I mean there was them that spent all their money in the pub. That was the unfortunate part.

There was a row of houses in Grafton Street. Mr Jarman's was about the middle. He used to talk to my mother when he came for his pension. He told my mother one day, he said his wife stood out on the step – you know, they used to come out and fold their arms and look up and down Grafton Street – and a woman came up to her, put a baby in her arms and went. They never did find her. They brought this boy up. Oh, he did turn out a lovely boy. He was a real gentleman. He went into the army in the First World War and the army found out who he was.

You can tell what a lovely family they were to have brought him up. But they were in the Boroughs. That was the kind of families we had in the Boroughs.

(Miss Lucy Starmer was Postmistress of the Grafton Street Post Office)

To me, memories of Scarletwell Street were good in respect of good neighbours, always willing to help each other. Mucking in spirit and all that. When you talk about the conditions it was shocking. I honestly don't know how some of the women survived down there. 'Cause for a woman it must have been a hard life, a very hard life. They used to have the children at home. There were no maternity hospitals and that, you had them upstairs in the bedroom. I mean, you hadn't got the facilities, you hadn't got hot water systems like you got now. You'd got a toilet about ten yards up the garden and you had to carry a bucket of water with you every time you went up there. You imagine going up there with about a foot of snow and ice, to go to the toilet. It must have been hard for them. It was a regular occurrence there for suicides, mainly women. Not the men. The men seemed to be able to tolerate the life. I suppose quite a few of them, as long as they went up and had a couple of pints, they could get over it. But a woman had still got it. She'd still be looking at it in the house. The husband could go out and forget it for a time. It must have been a hard life. I know two or three down there that either tried to gas themselves or threw themselves out of the bedroom window – but survived. They'd survive the gas because it was a penny in the meter. They hadn't got much money and probably the gas would run out before anything serious happened to them. If they jumped out of the bedroom window they'd probably finish up with a broken arm, or leg or collar bone. I don't actually remember any tragedies but a lot went on down there. I think it was a good thing when they cleared the area and rebuilt it. Because it was the buildings. It was a depression come from the buildings themselves. I'm not saying that you expect luxury, but if some of the children and that could go back to them... I certainly wouldn't want them to live in it, but I should like them just to see it. They'd be more grateful for what they've got now and appreciate it more.

(Reg Tero).

Right down where there used to be St. Andrew's Church, they bull-dozed that down and put new houses. They swept it clean and the people were moved out to Kings Heath, which, of course, won a national prize for being the best laid-out scheme in the country, at one stage. It cleared out the Boroughs but, I hesitate to say, it created more Boroughs.

(Ex-Detective Chief Inspector George Harding).

It didn't change 'til after the last war. Before, it was just the same, everybody helped each other, but since the war, it's all been grab, grab, grab. Nobody seems to want to help each other now.

(Alf Humphrey).

Cyril Benton: I think it stayed pretty well as it was until the demolition came. New people came, obviously, but some of the people spent all their life there. My wife spent all her childhood there and, a few doors away, was her mother's sister family. Everyone knew everyone else along there and it stayed like that until they were dispersed by compulsory purchase and demolition.

Richard Foreman: How did people react to that?

Cyril Benton: I think they reluctantly accepted it. My in-laws lived in their house for donkey's years. Originally they rented it, then they bought it from the landlord who couldn't really afford to keep up with repairs on the property. So they bought it as sitting tenants. When the compulsory purchase order came, they accepted that. They got a hell of a lot more than they paid for the property, as you can imagine, because it had a present day valuation. Father-in- law died, but Mother-in-law moved up to Lakeview in a council flat. I think, at that stage, (she was) quite happy to be out of there to something better.

Richard Foreman: People had quite mixed feeling about it.

Cyril Benton: You know it's got to go. don't you?

REG TERO'S STORY

My story begins during my childhood. In the late '20's. At the time I was living at number 99 Scarletwell Street in what they called a 'jerry-built' house. The underground kitchen was unusable except for a water tap with an old yellow stone sink. The living room at street level also contained the gas cooker and the front door opened from the street.

The first bedroom was very small; in this bedroom slept mother, father, two sisters and myself. The second bedroom, above, was unusable and when it rained father had to put buckets up there to catch the water.

How I remember Scarletwell Street was the unemployment. (Probably two out of every three homes). The Good Samaritans came round with clothes and shoes for the unemployed families. Everyone knew when a girl had Samaritan shoes for they were lace-up high boots. But these people carried out some very good work.

A fish and meat van came round every week and gave their wares free to the unemployed families. We were fortunate to have a father in work although even a man at work had very little to spare. Our only holiday was a one day a year at Margate on a cheap train trip.

Saturday night on the Mayorhold when the pubs turned out was highlighted by small groups of drunken men settling their differences with a fist fight; no knives, bottles etc. in those days. We, as children, remember it more for the fun we had playing in the 'Orchard'. This was a recreation space in Bath Street with swings, slides, Maypole etc. and below this was the Borough Yard. This is where we get our name 'The Borough Boys'. The Borough Boys came from Castle Street, Bath Street and Scarletwell Street.

At Christmas Eve, when we were all in bed, Father Christmas would come round to the doors of the unemployed, with a parcel for each child.

I was 7 years of age then and we moved to 28 Horsemarket. Here a new life began for all of us. A larger house, four bedrooms, front room, living room and kitchen and when we had electric light put in around 1936, it became a dream home to us children. After all, we only had to go two yards to the lavatory (as it was called in those days) instead of 20 yards, as was the case in the old Scarletwell Street.

I remember the Vicar of St. Katharines had a daughter named Eileen Pitt-Marston. When she was over here from America, she always visited the sick. One lady in St. Mary's Street who laid ill with TB was given a wireless by Miss Pitt-Marston, so that she could end her days with a little comfort. Her father, the Reverend Pitt-Marston, always called in the Red

Lion after Sunday morning service for his glass of beer.

There were four pubs that time in Horsemarket, the Red Lion, corner of St. Katherines Street, the Kings Arms, corner of King Street, New York Tavern opposite and the Coopers Arms corner of Castle Street.

In the late 1930's the shop on the corner of St. Mary's Street was taken over by Mr Berry as a cycle shop. At the same time, the Northampton Wireless Relay was born. This copany took over a showroom belonging to the Augustine Garage next door to us.

This was something new to working class families. It consisted of a speaker and a two station switch fitted to the window frame. The stations were then relayed from their station in Horsemarket to homes all over the town. The cost was two shillings a week until the speaker was paid for and then it was reduced to one shilling and threepence. As the station was next door to us, the first one was tried out in our house and so we had the first wireless relay. This became a wonderful service to those living alone. The first speakers were made by Mr Smith in his woodwork supply shop further up Horsemarket.

We had our fish and chip shop owned by Mr Warren. A grocery shop (Mr Amos), garment and wool shop (Mrs Gardener). Paper shop (Mr England). Baker shop (Mr Green). Another grocery shop (Mr Boys) where the cat sat in the window on top of the sweets.

In 1937 we moved further down to number 22, as the Relay required our house for expansion. Opposite was Latimer and Crick, corn merchants, and the Spencer Temperance Hotel. The rich cattle men from Ireland used to stay at this hotel while they visited Northampton Cattle Market.

George Civil had his first new premises in St. Katherines Street about this time. Us lads would be employed there Saturday mornings scraping the tins and jars of wet mixtures and putting them in bags for him to sell on his market stall.

To recall everything of those hard, but happy days of my childhood would take another ten sheets, so I will close now, in the year 1939, and war has now been declared.

CHAPTER 1 – 'HANKING AND PANKING'
– Memories of Childhood, Parents and Grandparents

John Stevens, born in 1901 (with Richard Foreman and Kate Wills).

John Stevens : I was born in my father's mother's home, 60 Bath Street. Very shortly after that (my parents) removed to Bell Barn Gardens. We lived there for a period, until my next sister was born. I was the first of the bunch and she was 18 months younger than me. We then removed to 13 Crispin Street, the middle (house) of a block of four.

The people who lived in one were named Richards. The people who lived next door were named Thompson. There lived in the next house, for a short time, a man who carried on two occupations. He was a glazier and a hairdresser. He had over his door: 'Suffer little children to come unto me and have their hair cut'. Now, he didn't live there very long. Shortly after that, a family named Simmonds came. The next house was empty, just a playground for kids to be in. It had been a shop and it had been occupied by the Haddon family. You know, the Haddon family, florists and greengrocer and fruiterers. The next house beyond that was occupied by a family named Turlands. There used to be other Turlands, who lived in Crispin Street on the opposite side of the road, and they were wood merchants. When I say wood merchants, I mean firewood merchants. Used to buy sleepers from the railway and chop them up into faggots, which we used to buy in those days.

My great grandfather lived with us for a period. He was 80 in 1914. He was a handsewn shoe maker. They used to work with a shoe on a last, in the clamp which they held with their knees, sewing. My mother used to make his wax ends for him, which were the threads fastened with the wax instead of the needle, which he passed through the holes...

Richard Foreman : Was he still working at the age of 80?

JS : I'm talking before 1914 but he virtually worked until his eyesight absolutely went.

My grandmother, who was his daughter, used to tell me things about her father. That was my great grandfather. She used to say to me that he used to go to Raunds to fetch his work, once a week. Raunds is 15 miles from Northampton. Used to push a three-wheel wicker barrow, with his last week's work in it, on a Monday morning, to Raunds. Collect his money and his next week's work and bring that home, which meant that the whole of Monday was taken up with that journey, walking the 15 miles. My grandmother used to say to me, "If he weren't home by 6 o'clock, Johnny, I knew where he were. He were in the 'World's End'," – and I wondered where the 'world's end' was, you see. That's the sort of thing people did in those days. Then, of course, the family grew and some way had to be found for grandfather to be turfed out. Where he went I don't know. But he was still with us. We still kept in contact with him 'til he died.

RF: What were your parents' occupations?

JS: My father was a shoe operative. My mother never worked after she was married. She had seven children by the time she was 34. My father was killed in the First World War. I had one brother and five sisters.

RF: Can you remember anything about your father's work?

JS: Oh yes. I can tell you this. He used to start work at 7.30 in the morning and work until 6 at night, but they had an hour's dinner break. He worked at Marlowes which was in Countess Road.

Kate Wills : Did he work on Saturday?

JS: Oh yes. Everybody worked on Saturday mornings. See, there were four boot and shoe factories over that side of the river. And it was fairly labour intensive you know, the boot trade was. It was quite a procession when they were coming home at dinnertime. Many women went and met their men to make sure they got their money before they went in the Spotted Dog. These are things we can laugh about, but they weren't laughable for those people, you know. My father's money at that time was thirty-five shillings a week.

KW : Do you know what the rent was?

JS : I think it was four and six.

RF : As a child, did you manage to earn ha'pennies and farthings now and again?

JS : My father was one of five sons and two daughters and they all worked in the boot and shoe factory except the eldest son. 'Course they used to come home, 6 o'clock, wanting their meals. I used to go from my grand-mother's to the Mayorhold, fetch some chitterlings from Pontins, or to a fish and chip shop at the bottom of Campbell Street and get some cow heel, and all this sort of thing.

RF : So you'd earn your money through doing errands?

JS : Yes. I always used to get a ha'penny a week for sharpening the knives and forks and cleaning them up on a Saturday morning. I used to do the knives and forks and my sister used to do the spoons. We got a ha'penny each for that.

Len Riley (with Kate Wills and Jon Small).

Len Riley was born in Herbert Street in 1904.

Len Riley : My father, he was a clicker in the boot trade. Mother didn't have a job, she merely looked after the family and we were a large family too. I was the eldest of 8. After me there's Alf, Florrie, Edie, Edna, Perce, Reg and Sid. And that's the family.

Kate Wills : What do you remember about the house?

LR : Well, you'd got to remember that in those days, money was very tight. And you had a scrubbed table and a hand-turned sewing machine. Five or six chairs and struggle how you like round the table for your meals.

KW : Did you all fit round the table?

LR : Not always. I always sat on the little table on the sewing machine. I'd got a lot of dislikes in food. When Mother used to make a stew, which I couldn't eat, Mother used to cook me something separate and I sat on my own.

KW : What sort of thing did you get up to as a child?

LR : Oh everything. You name it – we got up to it! It was very rare that I was in. I was either out playing or off on the scrounge somewhere. Knocking people's door and hiding. Tie a bit of cotton on the door knockers and get the other side of the road. They couldn't see you in the dark. Then knock the door. The people come out, couldn't see anybody, shut the door. Soon as they'd gone in, 'tap, tap, tap,' (laughs). And another game (was) to put a half a crown sugar bag on the pavement. Some old lady come along – "Oooh'." 'Chhh' – it was gone.

Jon Small: On a bit of string?

LR: Yes.

KW: It's called making your own amusements isn't it?

LR: Well, you had to. Used to play with cigarette cards a lot – all sorts of games we had with those. And then in their season – bowling hoops in the spring, marbles in the summer.

KW: Snowballs in the winter?

LR: Oh yes. Pack (the snow) up on somebody's door then rap the door – it fell in! (laughter). There wasn't anything to keep you in. We used to clear off, our gang, very often on a Saturday morning and go out in the country and live off the land and get back Sunday night. Nobody worried.

KW: What, scrumping apples?

LR: Yes. Chewing swedes, turnips. In their season, blackberries, crab apples. When wheat was growing, ears of wheat – chew them.

KW: What did you do when the weather was wet?

LR: The weather didn't worry us at all. I can only remember, once, we decided to walk the 'three eights'. That was from here to Weedon, Weedon to Towcester and from Towcester home. Twenty-four miles. And one of our mates was trailing behind. The sole come off his shoe and we tied it up with string 'til we got home, and it was raining at the time. We were all wet. Unfortunately, he caught pneumonia, and died a week later.

Elsie Bull (with Angela Connor).

Elsie Bull was born in 1904, in St. Mary's Street.

Elsie Bull: My father was a builder. Do anything in the building line. He worked for himself.

Angela Connor: Your mother?

EB: She didn't go to work. They didn't go to work those days because they'd got a big family and couldn't go on working. (They) wouldn't have them in the shops. No shopkeeper would employ a married woman. If (married women) wanted to earn a few shillings, used to do washing for half a crown a week for people.

I had seven sisters and one brother. A big family, but we was well looked after. We was always clean and tidy. And I'm proud of my parents – although they were strict I don't think the discipline hurt us.

We always used to know what we was going to have for breakfast. We used to get up about 7, have egg Mondays, bacon Tuesday, Wednesdays we'd have porridge . . . We used to know what we were going to have for meals. We were well fed. But, I don't mind telling you, some of the children were very poor. They hadn't got enough for a pair of shoes or anything. They used to have free (school) meals, some of them, and Good Samaritan clothes. Red dresses and all that. We never used to have anything like that, 'cause we was all bought up respectable and disciplined. 'Course – shall we say – my people were in a better position.

Used to play with Marjorie, Doctor Stone's daughter. (She) lived in Horsemarket. Horsemarket, those days, was all shopkeepers' daughters and doctors' daughters and all that kind of thing. We used to have some lovely parties. It's the only time the parlour had the plants taken out and we were let in there to play. I used to have to play the piano. 'Do you know the Muffin Man' and that sort of thing. And for musical chairs. We used to have some really lovely times – well, we thought they was. Postman's Knock along the passage with a boy! You can laugh, but we'd got nothing else, had we?

These people (we knew) used to have a big shop in the Drapery and they used to have a big William Pear tree in the back of their house. The fronts of the houses those days were like hotels. It wasn't like they are now. You know what I mean – space. All these windows and things. They'd got maids and all that sort of thing. Doctor Stone had a maid.

AC: In the Boroughs it was different, wasn't it though?

EB: That was Boroughs.

AC: That was the Boroughs as well?

EB: Yes, when I was a child.
Used to have to go and see our granny every Sunday night before we went to chapel. She lived on the Mayorhold, in a big house on the corner of Bath Street. She used to give us a farthing each to spend, but we couldn't spend it until Monday. It's wrong to spend money on Sunday, you see – that's how we were brought up.

We used to go to Silver Street, start with that, with a farthing's worth of toffee. We had nice sweets for a farthing, we had as much as a quarter, nearly. I used to be fond of bon- bons and 'ju-ju's' – you know those?

AC: Did you go to a particular shop for them?

EB: Oh yes. Spencers over the road, next to the clinic in King Street. A special shop for it. She was a nice old lady. She was clean – the other people used to lick their fingers and all that. We was a bit particular, as children, about that sort of thing. It was Mother, she was to blame.

AC: What pocket money did you have, apart from what your granny gave you?

EB: We used to have a penny a week (for) our allowance.

AC: Was that from your father?

EB: Yes. I used to waste mine, to go to the pictures for a penny.

AC: Did you earn any pocket money at all? Did you do any little jobs?

EB: No. Wasn't allowed to, you see. Mother always said there was a time and a place for that. Of course, I used to have to spend most of my time over at the chapel playing piano. I started the piano when I was 5, so I can play pretty fair. I used to play for social evenings. It caused a lot of jealousy between the family, because I got out more. I got a few more dresses than they did.

AC: Can you remember the games you played as a child?

EB: We played skipping, tip-tap... I had a diabolo. I wasn't very good with that. High ackee. Swinging on lamp-posts. The old gas lamps used to have two arms. We used to have some rope from the orange boxes at the fruit shop – ha'porth of rope. We used to tie it on and swing round the lamp-post.

(At) Beckets Park, used to be a nice meadow called Cow Meadow. In the bottom of it there used to be a bridge over the river. Used to be grass over there. Used to go and take a bottle of kali water and a picnic. Well, now they've flooded it – made it into another pool. I used to fancy my chance then. I suppose you'd call it sports. Used to have rowing boats out for a shilling, along the Nene. Well, I could row. I used to feather. So we used to go (on) Sunday afternoons, unbeknown to my mother. We saved up sixpence of our money and we used to go (rowing) up to the locks – the Britannia. We hadn't used to go over the locks or anything like that, but used to turn around and turn back, you see. Dad used to get a wagonette – like a brake – a smaller one – and the whole family used to go out for the day when it was a holiday day. He would drive the horse. He used to take us to Syresham, near Brackley. We used to hire the horse from Moss's in Spring Gardens. There used to be all stables where the horses were kept.

AC: What was Christmas like?

EB: Oh, lovely... Sixpenny toy out of Woolworths. I bought Mother a platter flower pot, sixpence. Nothing inthe store was over sixpence. In Gold Street.

AC: Was it a big family affair?

EB: Yes. We slept two in a bed, you know – well, we was asleep in the room next to Dad and Mother. The two youngest, you see. We used to hang our stockings up and have a new penny put in, an orange, an apple, a few treats and everything else. One night I happened to wake up when Dad was filling my stocking. I says: "Dad, you said it was Father Christmas..." He said: "Shh, Mabel'll hear you. You mustn't tell her." So I never said anything and went to sleep again. I wanted to empty mine, but I didn't.

Mr John Short (with Richard Foreman).

Mr Short was born in November 1906, at his parents' home, 46 Bearward Street, but his family moved house shortly after that.

John Short: It was many years afterwards that I learned that I was born in Bearward Street. All I can tell you is it had a sort of double door, a big door, painted brown. I should imagine it was three or four bed-rooms by the look of it.

Richard Foreman: Were your parents both working?

JS: Well, in those days, very few women worked. My father used to keep a job about a year or so, then he'd change it to perhaps a few coppers more a week. I remember him earning twenty-eight shillings a week. I had three older sisters and they worked in a closing factory. I used to go up to meet them out of work on a Saturday morning and we had to go and meet my Dad after work to get his money. Otherwise he'd have spent it in the pub. Or most of it.

He worked in Gold Street... a big ironmongers. He worked in Woolmonger Street in the steel warehouse. Then he had a job at

Mannings Brewery. That's near the Castle Station. And the last job he had: he worked at Colyers. A packer in a boot factory. Packing the boots in cases. During the time he was there, he died. That was 1916. I was 9 years old.

RF: Are your family a Northampton family?

JS: I think all the children were born in Northampton. My father was born in Wellingborough and my mother was born in Banbury. They met in Daventry. What my father was doing in Daventry, I don't know, but my mother was working in the kitchens of a hotel at the time. They lived in Daventry for a time, I think, and then they came to Northampton. It appears that they lived all over the town: Kingsthorpe, Far Cotton, St. James and in the centre. I think the rents of houses had a lot to do with where people lived. I think my Dad used to change his job according to where he lived.

RF: Where do you first remember?

JS: Far Cotton. We lived in a house in Main Road, Far Cotton. And I remember it was before I used to wear trousers. We didn't used to change into trousers until I was about 3. And they didn't cut boys' hair until I was about 3. I remember seeing a photo of myself with long curls.

(We) moved back from Far Cotton to Little Cross Street and we lived there for about six weeks and then we moved to Fort Street.

I've got happy memories of holidays. We never went away for holidays but we used to go for country walks. We used to take a bottle of tea and some bread and butter or bread and jam – it wouldn't be butter, it'd be margarine – and go to Harlestone Firs. Walked up there. And of course, there was no houses between Spencer Bridge Road and Harlestone Firs. Only the village of Dallington.

We used to go to Foot Meadow, catching train names. We used to climb up on the railway bridges, over the wall through the meadow. I remember being pulled up by a railway man from off this bridge, me and another boy. We were taken to the station and given a good talking to. I don't think I ever got up on the bridge again. 'Course it was only a yard away from the wheels of the engines.

We used to go to the Orchard, on the swings, in Bath Street, quite a lot. Then there was the Burying Ground in Chalk Lane and Doddridge Street. That had swings and see-saws, maypole... And Paddy's Meadow, down the bottom of Grafton Street. If you looked over the bridge on the Spencer

Bridge Road, you could always see dead cats and dead dogs in the river. Always. People used to take then down, put it into a bag and throw it over into the river.

We used to go scrumping. It's now Gladstone Road. There was gates across and beyond that was all smallholdings, fruit trees, orchards. So we used to go there scrumping on occasions. We was chased several times with the policemen. They didn't frighten anybody, but you kept clear of them. You didn't want to get caught. Because, if he caught you, he'd perhaps give you a clout round the ears with his gloves or something like that. Well, we didn't want that. They didn't take many boys in if they caught them scrumping. They only give them a jolly good telling off.

I remember too, when I was a boy, it was horse traffic. Very little motors. And up Marefair and Gold Street it was all cobbles each side of the tramlines. Very often, horses used to fall down. The driver would kneel on its head until it was unhooked in the shafts. Until it was free, you see, and able to get up. If we heard one falling down, we always ran to see what was happening. And with carts and horse drawn vehicles, we used to get on the back axle, underneath the cart and have a ride.

RF: Wasn't that a bit dangerous?

JS: I suppose it was. But there was no motors about. If we see any boys doing that, if we see them from the path, we'd shout to the driver: "Whip behind!" and he used to whip behind!

And then we used to have a good old time, Wednesday afternoons, visiting the slaughterhouse in Bath Street. We used to help pull the bullock in from the loose boxing to the slaughterhouse. Perhaps half a dozen (children) helping to pull the bullock in. There'd be two men. The slaughterhouse was behind the butcher's shop in Bath Street. And the butcher's name was Bullock! That was on the other corner to the Sportsman's Arms.

During my schooldays I used to help a man sell skimmed milk on Sundays. It was a penny a pint – about half price to the ordinary milk. On Sundays it was used to make the Yorkshire pudding. We sold a lot of milk.

We used to do errands for anybody on the street. You'd perhaps get a ha'penny or a penny and that was quite useful. Anybody that wanted errands doing, they used to go to the front door – and any boy or girl going by, they'd ask them: "Would you run down to Sanders for me, my duck?" They'd bring the goods back whatever it was; a quarter of tea or perhaps a bag of sugar and they'd perhaps give you a ha'penny. Well, that was worth doing. Sometimes you didn't get anything. If you was lucky you got a ha'penny or a penny.

I had a go at selling 'Echoes' and I was no good at (it). That was when the 'Chronicle and Echo' were separate papers. I used to go with a boy who was very good at selling 'Echoes' and he'd give me a dozen to get on with. He'd sell 20 where I sold about 2. So I couldn't carry on like that. I didn't earn any money! So I got a job at Jeyes the chemist in the Drapery.

RF: What age would you have been?

JS: 12. I went each Monday, Tuesday, Thursday and Friday. I went from 5 o'clock to half past seven. Saturdays I went in the afternoon, at 1 o'clock 'til about 5 o'clock. I used to do that sweeping up and any little job that came along. And I had five shillings a week – which was a big help to my mum. I was there two years.

RF: Presumably, that and your sister's earnings supported the family after your Dad died. Did your mother get any kind of benefit?

JS: No. No assistance in those days. I think there was a Poor Law, but she wouldn't have got anything with the income she would have got from my sisters.

During the time I was at Jeyes, I was also a choirboy at St. Peters in Marefair for four years. St. Peters; the clergyman also served Upton Church, on the Weedon Road. There was a nice little church there, very small. We used to go up there Sunday afternoons and do the singing business.

RF: How did you get out there?

JS: Walk. There was no other means. I think that was before buses started.

A friend of mine lived on Bristol Street. They used to sell vegetables and toffee apples for a ha'penny each. From the front room. Wasn't furnished see? And I've been down into their cellar. Each side of it was stacked up with old iron; chains, nuts and bolts. Anything metal – it was in that cellar. I should think when they cleared out it must have been two or three tons of things that his father had picked up on his travels.

He was an outside porter. He used to work from the Castle Station and I believe he'd either a letter or postcard to come to his house to say 'Meet Mr. So-and-So at Castle Station'. And they used to meet commercial travellers. He'd perhaps have a couple of baskets, skips to put on his handcart and go up the town and stop outside the line that the commercial traveller was selling – say, a tailors, and he'd perhaps do 2 or 3 tailors in a day. And that was his job. Wheeling along the traveller's samples.

That was the first part of the war. Half-way through, the railway took him on as a driver of parcel vans. They used to go all over the town collecting parcels. It was a busy trade in those days.

Me and Tom, that was his son, used to go out with him round St. James End after school hours. There were perhaps a dozen factories in St. James. We used to go to all of them. And perhaps you'd get 100 parcels in from one factory. Pair of boots. Two pairs of boots. Or perhaps half a dozen pairs in some parcels. They went by rail – there was no road transport. When we got back we used to unload the van. It all went into the parcel office. And that was him finished. He used to unhook the horse and the parcel van was left at the Castle Station. The stabling for the parcel horses was in St. Peter's Street, behind St. Peter's Church. We used to go along with his father to stable the horse. I can remember the smell of the stable now. That was the first stable I went in. They were nice, though, kept clean and well looked after.

But the railway had a monopoly on that business. Collecting parcels from the factories. I used to collect parcels for a cycle shop on the main road in St. James, too. That was before I was 12. I didn't get anything for it. It was only just for something to do after school. That was about 1916/1917 time.

I was about 7 years old when the First World War started. I can remember the day. I was going down Chalk Lane. There was a newsagents at the bottom and as I crossed the road it said on a placard: 'England declares war on Germany'.

During the war I used to fetch coal from Hughes. A coal firm named Hughes. That's where St. Peter's Way is now. The gas company was there and they had a rail line running into the gas company. A branch of it ran into this firm, Hughes. It was one and sixpence a hundredweight. We used to have to pay three ha'pence an hour for the handcart. We used to hire a handcart. We could also get a bushel of coke for sixpence at the gasworks. And also get a bushel of logs from a place in Broad Street, Finnegans.

Kit Lack and Elsie Allen (with Richard Foreman).

Kit Lack was born at 17 Compton Street in 1911, and Elsie Allen at number 53 in 1912. Kit Lack's father worked on the railway, but died at the age of 41.

Kit Lack: He hadn't worked for 5 years because of his heart. He had heart trouble from the army. Our mother was left with 5 of us and she had nine and sevenpence a week from the Soldiers'... Then they brought the Widows' Pension in for ten shillings a week and she used to worry herself that she hadn't got to have that, that's the other money...

Richard Foreman: Can you remember your grandparents?

KL: They lived in 22 Compton Street, I can remember our pap used to walk to Duston, there and back, when he was 82. He used to be in a shoe factory.

RF: (to Elsie Allen) What do you remember about number 53?

Elsie Allen: The only thing I can remember is being upset as a tiny kid. There was a terrific fight in the street with two women. I was in my nightdress and I run downstairs 'cause it frightened me. I can remember our Dad picking me up and putting me on his shoulder. And that's the memory I've got of that place.

You see we moved. Our mother opened a shop and she'd got (it) when the war broke out. I was 2. The shop was in Compton Street, 29. A bit of grocery ... and toffee apples. It started with toffee apples. She'd got five shillings and she went out, brought some sugar, apples, sticks... Our Dad said to her when he came home: "How many toffee apples did you sell?" She said: "Sixty." She'd just made the five shillings, a penny a toffee apple.

When the war was on she sold all the sugar out. She went to Tommy Needles and asked him if she could have a bit of sugar. He said: "What have you done with the other?" She said: "Sold it." He said: "Did you know war's broke out? You won't get any more. How are you selling it?" She said she used to weigh the sugar and put it in the bag. He said: "You mustn't do that! You must weigh the bag with your sugar. You'll never make any profit!"

RF: What did your father do?

EA: He'd got a good job in a shoe factory but I don't know where it was. He needn't have gone (to fight in World War I) but all his pals had gone so he volunteered. Now when he come home on leave, he didn't want to go back again. He ripped all his papers up and our mother had to stick them together again. He wouldn't have gone to France, he would've gone to

India, but he had fever from the innoculations. He was so ill in hospital he come home on leave. He went back, straight to France, and was killed. He was only up 8 months from calling up and being ill (to) getting killed.

There was this woman in Grafton Street wanted to adopt our Bill and another woman who took to me. Our mother said: "No. I'm not going to part with either of them. They're mine. I'm keeping them."

RF: Can you remember your grandparents?

EA: Only my grandmother. She lived in Monks Pond Street.

KL: Our mother loved working. Washing, ironing, minding children – she used to take them to the pictures and leave us with our dad when we was little, 'cause she minded them to get a bit of money. And washing. I'd see her with her two baths. On this. In this. Blue them and starch them...

RF: Can either of you remember any games you might have played in your spare time, as children?

KL: Well, we used to go 'up the top' and play 'Hop Across' and try and knock the other one down. Some would come this way, and you going that – and you've got to hop and try and knock them over.

EA: Marbles, hopscotch, whip and top, high ackee, hot can...

RF: Hot can? What was that?

EA: On a cold night, you're out playing in the cold and the boys come along with a can with some rag in. Lit. "Warm your hands! Want a warm?"

RF: So you'd warm your hands around the can.

EA: A rope on a lamp-post and... bump, bump, bump. You'd squeal like hell if anybody hit you, but then you bumped yourself going round the lamp-post.

RF: Did you go any farther afield than Compton Street?

KL: No. We used to go up Abington Park when we was away from school.

Used to take our tea.

EA: At nights, not too late, but on dark nights – we'd lay some games up the street 'cause the lamps were on. Annoying somebody, I expect. Round the lamp-post. Boys would come along and want a warm.

(On an) icy day us girls would make a slide. We'd have a nice steady slide and the boys would come along and take it over. Then we'd get another slide and, as soon as we'd got it going, they'd take it over. Still, I don't know whether they were good old days. They were good in some ways. They were safer.

Mr & Mrs Jim and Eileen Allard (with Richard Foreman).

Jim Allard: I was born in 1913, May 8th, at 93 Horsemarket. My father and mother kept that as a fishmonger's shop. They kept it over 50 years. Belonged to my grandfather before that. He were a horse-slaughterer by trade. My parents were horse-slaughterers for years. That's how my father learned his job as a vet. He used to cut them up.

My father was an old man when I was born. They'd call my father 'The Sherriff'.

Richard Foreman: Why?

JA: Because he was so domineering. Wanted everything doing his way. He used to sit for hours on the Mayorhold, on a handtruck. My grandfather were the same.

Eileen Allard : His name (was) Bill Allard. When he was asleep the kids used to go and tip his truck up and he used to go loopy. They used to play him up.

JA: He could do a bit of hawking. I used to go with him. Yelvertoft and that way, Crick, Long Buckby...He used to get drunk.

RF: Did he travel with a horse and cart?

JA: Yes. 'Nugget' he called the horse. He was a nugget and all. He always used to hit him up front. He'd never hit him behind, he always used to touch him with the whip up front. But he wouldn't go no faster up a hill than what he would down.

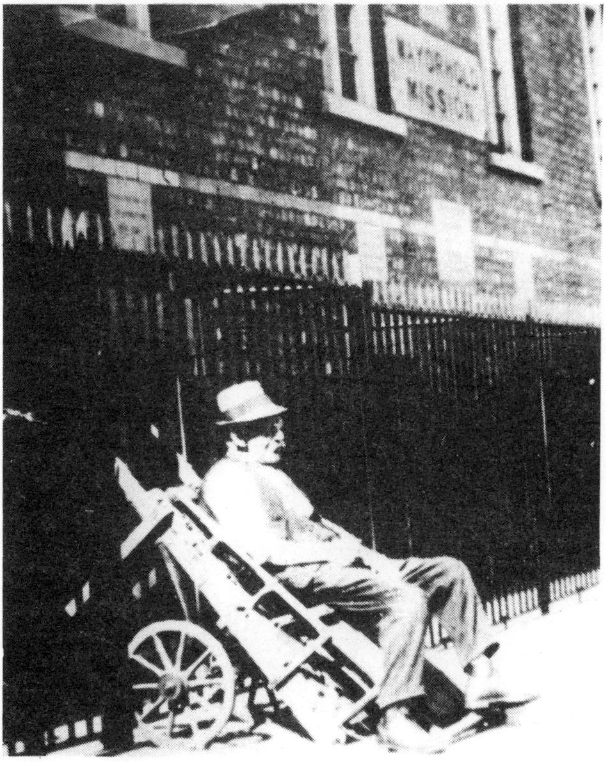

'The Sherriff' outside the Mayorhold Mission

RF: He had a will of his own?

JA: Yes You could lay into him, do what you liked –

EA: But he knew all the stopping places.

RF: Your parents took over the fishmongers' shop. What do you remember about that time?

JA: Mother was selling herrings seven for sixpence and kippers three ha'pence a pair. It were a struggle to get them bought and a struggle to get them sold.

You couldn't get a lot of stuff. Anything you want – wait! Because mother wouldn't have anything. Only special. It'd got to be right for mother. Herrings, seven for sixpence. You used to have to squeeze them to get the hard roe or soft roe or whatever they wanted. We used to go down the fishmarket – which were at the station then – about 5 or 6 in the morning. Go to school and get a good spanking, 'cause my… boots were dirty.

RF: Did you help out in the shop?

JA: Oh yes. Me and my sisters all picked mussels then. Skin rabbits…

RF: How many sisters did you have?

JA: Ginny, Florrie, Violet and Lil. Four girls and one boy. (I was) the youngest. Had quite a good childhood. Wasn't very hard living.

Bill Coulson (with Alan Williams).

Bill was born in 1915, the son of a shoe worker.

Bill Coulson : Our (home) conditions varied considerably with the shoe industry. Often they went on what was known as short time working – three days a week, which of course greatly reduced the family income. But immediately that was announced, Mother would send me up to the paper shop to cancel the papers (and) to the dairy to reduce the milk. She always kept a good store cupboard when we were slightly more flush. So we were able to survive quite well for a few weeks, with a few cutbacks.

Alan Williams: As a child, where and what games did you play?

BC: Mostly (we played in) Miller's Meadow. We played such things as hide-and-seek, kiss chase (laughs) – I soon became well-versed in that!

AW: Were you given any regular jobs as a child?

BC: At the age of 9, when my second sister started work, I had to take over household chores 'cause my mother said that she wasn't having any son of hers useless when (he) got married. So I had to learn everything in the house. By the time I was 12 I prepared and cooked a full Christmas dinner for seven people all on my own.

AW: Do you have any memories of the First World War?

BC: One particular thing stands out in my mind and that was when my father came home at the end of the War. I had never seen him. He walked in the living room door. Mother looked across the table at him and promptly fainted. I thought in some way that he was responsible (so I) shot round the table and started trying to knock my father about, small as I was. (Laughs).

Edna Brown (with Pat Edwards).

Edna Brown was born in 1917 at 24 Grafton place. Her father worked in the boot and shoe trade, at Church's in Duke Street.

Pat Edwards: Did your family have a sort of routine?

Edna Brown: Oh very much so. Yes.

PE: What did you have to do? What was your job?

EB: My job was to clean the stair rods or clean the cutlery. (My sister) would clean the cutlery one week and I would do the stair rods. Then, next week, we'd swap over. (That) included cleaning taps and all, any bit of brass. As we got older we had to learn to help with the ironing and we always took it in turns to wash up – one washed and one dried – dust, and all the little jobs like that. Fold the clothes as they were fetched in on washing day. We had to help do all that.

PE: Did your mother used to do any work for anyone else?

EB: She used to take washing in and, on one or two occasions, she'd look after someone's children. That was mostly only in the vicinity, they never came from any distance.

PE: Where would you go to play, outside the house?

EB: We played a lot in what was called the Stoneyard which was up Priory Street and round there, near Marlowe's shoe factory. We also played in the street a lot and down Paddy's Meadow. There used to be swings down there, but only the odd one or two. We played down there a lot in the summer, but in the winter we didn't go far. Mostly in the street. Victoria Park – we played a lot there in the summer. We used to paddle in the little brook and then we'd get a good hiding when we got home if our shoes and socks were wet.

PE: What kind of games did you used to play?

EB: Skipping, hopscotch... The road was all cobbley then – we'd pull a stone out of the road and play marbles. See how many marbles you could get in the hole. Then we'd have another game – we'd collect all the wire rings off the bundles of wood that Mum used to buy to start the fire off and we'd all take any old bits of toys that we'd got. We'd set them all out. Whoever caught one with a ring – that was theirs.

PE: Do you know what that one was called?

EB: Oh yes, 'The Old Firm'*. We'd swap cigarette cards and all that sort of thing. I think we used to give a cigarette card to have a go at this 'Old Firm'. Either that or marbles.

Mr & Mrs George and Phyllis Rolfe (with Louis Peters).

George Rolfe was born in Bearward Street, in 1921. Both he and his wife remember how strict their parents were.

PR: You daren't answer back.

GR: You get the blinking cuss straight on your blinking head. What you daren't! If you was having a dinner and your Mother wanted something from the shop, she'd say: "Oh, quick, nip down to the shop." If you said: "Wait a minute." ...Cor! That blinking stick. Ash stick. Hit you straight across the blinking head. You'd have to jump out quick and fetch it. There was no nonsense then.

PR: And if you left the table before Mother and Father got up, that was murder. You daren't get up.

GR: Even the boys used to have to do their turn in washing up. Used to go round.

PR: And clean the boots and shoes. One used to have to clean all of them and one used to wash the floors, one used to have to polish all the furniture and one used to have to empty the slops and make the beds.

**Boroughs children presumably took this name from an old fairground game, also known as 'The Old Firm'.*

GR: Do your whack.

PR: Boys and girls all the same. None of us got let off.

GR: Yes, they were strict then.

Louis Peters : Did you do any jobs as a lad to earn pocket money?

GR: You had to do a lot of different jobs. Like going to the gas house, fetching bags of coke for the stewed eel shop in Bearward Street and a fish and chip shop at the bottom.

LP: This was normal for a lot of youngsters then?

GR: Well, if you didn't get these errands, you'd get nothing. I mean, our pocket money was a penny a week. That's all we had. If you wanted any more you had to go and find some jobs. Used to run all the way home, from Spencer School to Bearward Street, pick the old truck up and run all the way down to the gas house 'fore they closed at 5 o'clock. Fetch the coke.

All the kids used to be together. A gang of girls and a gang of boys. Messed about (in) the Mayorhold and all that. Down the top of our street used to be what they called the Orchard, the swings and all that. The old Destructor used to back onto it from Castle Street. So if we were hanking and panking about or doing anything we shouldn't be doing and the police come, all we used to do (was) climb the railings into the old Destructor and come out into Castle Street.

LP: So you used to hang about in a gang in those days?

GR: Yes. Used to get different gangs: Green Street Gang, Scarletwell Street Gang, Bearward Street Gang... Used to have some battles! Oh yes, I've had my fair share of battles.

LP: How old would you have been then?

GR: Well, up to the 14 mark.

LP: Were there other areas of the town that you played in?

GR: Well there wasn't all that much about really when we was kids. All there was the YMCA in Grafton Street. Go and do a bit of boxing there if you wanted. And there used to be a bloke had a bit of a boxing school in the Bull and Butcher yard. Toddy Atkins. That's all. If not, you'd got nothing to do. You hadn't got no money for the pictures.

We used to go scrumping up Far Cotton. It was all fields up where the Queen Eleanor's Cross was. Used to be one big orchard, Cottrell's

Orchard. Used to go from one road to the other, the main road. The Newport Pagnell Road used to go across. So if you got trapped by the keepers, you'd got a chance to get out. Used to go up there a lot.

Used to go up Kings Heath. That used to be all fields and orchards and everything.

Joyce Hall.

Joyce Hall was born in 1923 at 21 King Street, the oldest of three children.

My mother was a housewife, principally, but she was a big worker at St. Katherine's church that was situated at the bottom of our yard where the St. Katherine's Memorial Square is now. She was enrolling member of the Mother's Union. She was on the speaker's list, so she went about various groups of the Mother's Union talking to them about various subjects.

My father was a 'principal' worker at Walker and Cooke in King Street. They were mainly cabinet makers, but also wheelwrights. They did a lot of metal work for county. Horses and traps, that sort of thing. (Also) he was a Diocesan Lay Preacher, attached to the Church of England. He went about taking services in the surrounding countryside where they hadn't got a vicar.

He wasn't actually going to go into the business. He and my mother were going to be missionaries and he was going to start some training towards the end of the First World War, but then he was blinded in one eye. He just came back and, in those days, they said that you'll just have to go into your father's business and do your church work as a part time thing.

He did the cabinet making and wheelwrighting. He also did little hand-trucks, (for) which the traders on the market square would come down on a Saturday morning. All the week it was open for hand-trucks to be hired out. It was about a penny an hour. We used to keep the 'truck book', as we called it. We children were in charge of that. But when my father was working they (the market people) used to go down the yard and he would hire the trucks out. As soon as he shut up business – about 5 or 6 in the evening – he'd come in. And the 'truck book' had to come in with us, because they were still out on hire and we children used to take over and book them in and out.

The traders would come Saturday morning, go down to the station, pick up the fresh fish, vegetables coming in from Covent Garden and wheel them up to the market. Probably keep the truck all day – probably had it for 8 hours, 8 pence at the end of the day – then bring the truck in. Now, some of them were such rogues that they would leave them on the market when they had finished. Often, on the Saturday night, the police would come and ring our bell – 10, 11 o'clock at night – and say: " Mr. Walker, one of your trucks has been left down on the market square. We have taken it off to the police station. Will you come up Monday morning and pick it up?" Then we used to have to pay a fine.

My father was such a lovable character and so easy going, he would never turn nasty with them. I never heard him say: "Well, you won't have one this week." Never. And this is why the business had gone down and down. I mean, he earned better money doing the traps for the country people. All their horses came down to the yard to be shod and he had rent from the ones that used to do the shoeing. My father used to repair all their lovely traps. You know, when they went hunting and the country people used to drive round the country lanes in those high traps with big wheels. Well, he used to charge for all those sorts of jobs. But, towards the end of her life, mother used to get a bit peeved, she used to say: "Well, we don't make anything letting trucks out, people letting you down." And father used to say: "Never mind. We're doing them a service." So this is why you end up with no money.

All night, every day of the week except Sunday, right through until about 11 o'clock at night, the yard was open for trucks to come in and out. If people wanted to move house they'd move with a truck, a lot of them, because they couldn't afford vans in those days – except for big furniture.

I think we children felt that we were expected to stay in in the evenings and help run up and down those stone steps. If my mother had been on all day looking after us, washing, ironing, she was absolutely flaked out but she still kept on cooking and feeding us.

My father was very friendly with the vicars at St. Katherines and they often had (their own) children. Because my father worked for them they used to pass on all the nice dresses. I can remember going to church and the people would come out to watch my father and my mother march we three children up the street and down. To look. Because you'd got perhaps a silk dress on or something, which to us was only second-hand and passed on. But it was so fantastic, we lived in a fairy world really. We didn't do it with any nastiness because they knew, as soon as we'd finished with them – the dresses – mother would go across and take them to them. They had our cast-offs. So this is how you lived. My father and mother were ever so poor.

There was a little bookshop in St. Giles Street, a Mr Arlidge, and when I was old enough, I was allowed to go there on a Saturday and help him deliver a few magazines in the town centre. I also went to music lessons on a Saturday morning. Most of our lives was connected with the church.

We belonged to the Girls' Friendly Society. We had to join that sort of thing, everything was involved with the church. That was the way we wanted it. We weren't forced to do it. We would, as we grew older, have to be Sunday School teachers. It was expected of us.

Ours was a sort of an 'open house'. Father was a kindly man. If they'd got any problem, they'd come and ring our bell. "Mr Walker, will you come and see so-and-so. They're ill," or: "My wife's gone off and left me." He'd go and talk to them and try to do the sort of counselling that probably Social Services do today. He was the one in the area they all used to run to.

They were so hard up, he would try and do something to bring them money or clothes. Children hadn't got shoes and socks to go to school in. He felt that this was something neighbours ought to do. He would go round to the lodging houses in Horsemarket, visit the men and see if there was anything they wanted and if they were all right.

We were brought up very strictly. We all went to bed at 7 or 8 at night. We weren't allowed to roam the streets. We would have our meal, help with the trucks, go to our one or two things at church and then in and to bed. We weren't allowed to do anything on a Sunday because it was our rest day, God's day. We weren't allowed even to pick up a bit of knitting. You went to church and sat and read a bit of good literature in the afternoon. That made us a little bit deceptive. Longing to get on to this bit of knitting, you'd go up to your bedroom and think: 'I'll fetch it out for half an hour.' Mother would call up: "What are you doing up there?" "Nothing. Just coming down."

You were allowed to go to a dance on a Saturday night when you were 17, but father used to say: "Come straight home." We used to have little Saturday night dances at St. Katherines church hall. It was just beginning, because the troops were moving into the area. 10 o'clock it would finish. Reasonable hours. Your boyfriend would walk you home and you soon had to come into the house. Well, this was just the beginning of where you started breaking away and things started to change.

Josephine Kent (with Julia Bush)

Josephine Kent was born in Bath Street in 1923. Her father was a boot and shoe operative. She had two brothers and three sisters.

Josephine Kent: We had our jobs. My father used to make a list and it was put on the wall on Monday. Your jobs were up there – what you had to do all week. And they were turned round.

It was like my mother had two families. She had four before the First World War and two afterwards. So there was a big gap. So it was usually me and my sister. We used to have to work out what we'd done then, at the end of the week, you had a ha'penny. That was your reward for a week's work.

You used to have to clean brasses, do a bit of ironing and, every night, we used to do a bit of mending. Or – one night it was sewing, another night it was knitting, another night it was embroidery. We used to have to do something every night.

We used to make our own clothes. Boys' trousers were made out of father's old trousers. Dresses were made out of mother's pinas. It done you in good stead when you was older. (You) could do all these things. That's the way it went and you never dreamt of saying 'no'. You just obeyed.

Julia Bush: Did the boys help in the house as well?

JK: Well, not really, in our home. As I say, the others were grown up when me and my sister were small. The only brother I can remember being younger went to the navy when he was 14½.

We had a lady living in Windsor Terrace. Her name was Mrs. Barker. She used to take in washing. Mabel Smith's washing, Mrs James' washing off the Mayorhold and Mrs. Amos' washing from Horsemarket. They all kept shops. I used to have to take the washing back to them people, collect the money and take it to Mrs. Barker.

JB: That's another job you had then.

JK: Oh yes, you had to work. You used to have a ha'penny for taking those three lots of washing.

I used to have an aunt lived next door but one, Aunt Lizzie. She never had any children and I used to do her errands all the week. On a Saturday I used to have a ha'penny and a bottle of ginger beer. She used to make this ginger beer. When I took it home, I could either have the ginger beer and I had to save the ha'penny – or I had the ha'penny and I never had the bottle of ginger beer. I often wondered, years later, what happened to those bottles of ginger beer that I never had!

You had to work for it, but you weren't allowed to spend needlessly. You always had to save. Didn't matter what we had given to us, we used to have to save half.

JB: Were your parents happy for you to play out in the street?

JK: Oh yes. Where we lived, Windsor Terrace, was a 'pudden-bag street' (ie. a cul-de-sac). We used to have wonderful fun when we was children. There was never any thoughts of anything being wrong, even when it was dark. You weren't allowed out late, 'cause you had to be in bed early, but there was no fear at all for children playing.

You didn't go out a lot in winter, 'cause it used to get dark early. We used to come home from school, then you had your tea and then we always had to have half hour music, then homework from school. If it was very dark, it was just too late to go out and play then. But in the summer months, when it was nice and light, you were allowed out 'til it got dark.

The playground that used to be down Bath Street – the 'Orchard' as we used to call it – there used to be an old man that looked after it. His name was Mr. Stroud. He lived in Silver Street. There was never any trouble down there with children. Don't matter how many children there was, he kept control and made sure nobody was bullied. He used to sit in a little hut at the top of the Orchard, and he used to tell stories. We used to sit round there and listen to him. He was a dear old man. I can see him now in his black overcoat and his cap. He was a very interesting old man.

JB: Was he retired?

JK: That's what his job was, to look after the children. To make sure the children didn't bully the little ones. He was a nice old man.

JB: Was he there every day?

JK: Oh yes, except Saturdays and Sundays.

Ron Draper (with Ron Johnson)

Ron Draper: I was born at home, 12 Bath Square, on 6th June, 1925. We used to have nurses come. Nurse Mossey delivered me, and I think, subsequent children.

Ron Johnson: Did Nurse Mossey do all the nursing?

RD: No, only delivering babies.

RJ: Were your parents born in Northampton?

RD: Oh yes, they were born in the Boroughs, my mother was born in Horsemarket I think. Although my Grandmother Hardwick – I'm going on hearsay here – originally lived up Manfield Hospital. They had to come out of that house so that Manfield Hospital could be built. She said it was that that sent her father to drink.

RJ: What was your father's occupation?

RD: He started out, like the rest of us in the town, as a shoe operative. He worked for a place called Branches in Henry Street and he got laid off. Well then he went to cattle droving. Used to follow the markets. My father used to go to every market in the county. Rugby Monday, Harborough Tuesday, here Wednesday, Banbury Thursday, Kettering Friday, here again Saturday. Every market round here he used to do. He used to work for Pierce, Thorpe Marriots – Auctioneers, but he also did freelance, working for different farmers. Used to have a man come from Sheffield, a man called Hibbert, he wouldn't have nobody but my father to tend his sheep in the market here. Used to get paid by the load – that's how he made a living. In latter years my father went to a farm in Castlethorpe. We got a lovely letter when my Dad died.

RJ: Can you remember your grandparents at all?

RD: I can remember most of them vaguely, and my Grandmother Hardwick, she lived to be a ripe old age. I remember her most. She lived in Bath Square as well, and before that she lived in Scarletwell Street. She used to talk to me, see she was very political my grandmother. Her idol was Margaret Bondfield and then in her mid-life another name used to crop up – Tony Lyons, I think he was a Labour man in the town before I took any interest in politics.

My Grandfather Hardwick was a watchmaker. He only used to do it like from his house, he didn't do it from a shop or anything. He used to know a lot about watches and clocks, in fact his sons had his tools handed down and the eldest son was apt to do it as well, also shoe mending.

RJ: Do you remember your grandparents on your father's side?

RD: Not so well, because my Grandmother Draper died quite young. She died in Scarletwell Street, left quite a few children, they had about ten.

BATH SQUARE AND THE 'ORCHARD' – EARLY 1930's

Two views of Bath square, showing Ron Draper and friends. (Below) with uncles Jack and George Hardwick.

(Above) In the Orchard. "Cricket's my game!"
(Below) Ron, with brother Ken and sister Shirley, at the back of Bath Square.

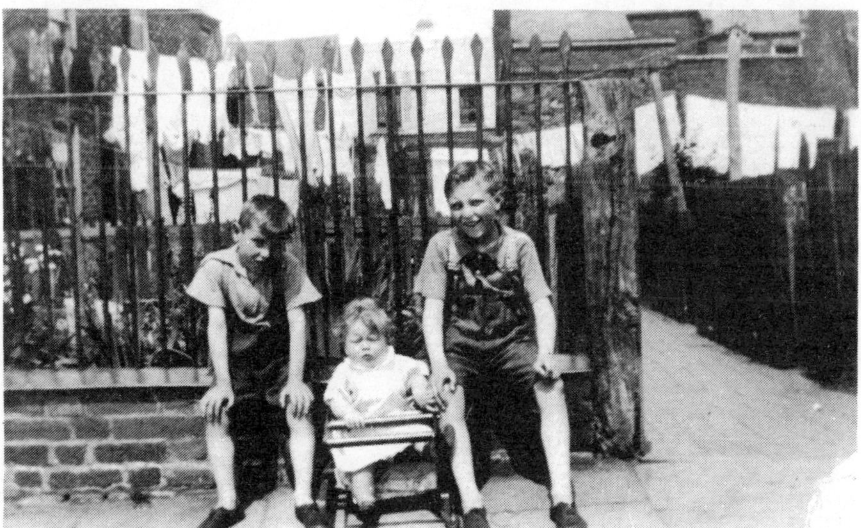

Scarletwell Street children (1920's)

Outside 24 Grafton Place (1930's)

BOB STANTON'S STORY

Bob Stanton was born in 1921, at number 4, The Mayorhold. From 1926 to 1931, his family lived at number 12.

I started school at St. Andrew's in 1926. The first morning we were given railway engines, carriages and trucks to play with. These were made at Winteringhams, a factory in St. Andrew's Street. In the afternoon – and each afternoon, in that first class – we had to lay down on rush mats on the floor. We were supposed to sleep for half an hour.

As part of our education in that class, we were each given a card about four inches square on which was a block capital letter, made of sandpaper. We had to keep rubbing our fingers over these letters, until we had learned same. When this was done, the card was changed for another letter. I think the moral was: the quicker you learned it, the less sore your finger became!

While at this school, in the early '30's, the airship R101 flew over and we were all sent into the playground to see it. It was housed at Cardington in Bedfordshire. A few years later, it crashed in France.

One highlight of the week was hurrying from school each Wednesday afternoon to look in Trasler's paper shop window and see what grisly picture was on the front of the Police Gazette. There was always someone hacked, chopped or done to death in some macabre way.

Another teatime to hurry home for was Friday's. You picked up a basin and a few coppers and went to the butchers' for hot faggots or chitterlings.

Although times were hard, there were times when you enjoyed yourself, as a youngster, without getting into a lot of trouble. Like – running your legs off with a hoop, playing whip and top, tip-cat or marbles. Sometimes I would get a pig's bladder from the slaughterhouse, blow it up and a few of us lads would go to the Racecourse and play football with it.

On winter or darker evenings, we would be running about with a handwarmer. This being a round tin (eg. a cocoa tin) with holes at both ends and burning rag inside. Talk about smoke! It used to nearly choke you sometimes. Another thing we did was to get a piece of black rubber which had been trimmed from a shoe sole. This you lit so that it smouldered. You can imagine the smell this caused. It was known as 'Stink Rubber'.

Every so often there were gang fights, so called, where gangs of lads from Scarletwell Street, Herbert Street, Bell Barn and Bath Street would charge each other on different nights. Although it was a bit hectic at times, no one got badly hurt and we were all mates again the next morning. These various gangs or groups formed up each polling day to go round the streets carrying placards in support of their choice and banging on large tins or anything. They would chant: "Vote, vote, vote for good old Maloney. Chuck old Renton in the cut." etc.

After the result of the election, that night, towards midnight, paper sellers would come haring down Bearward Street and across the Mayorhold shouting at the top of their voices, "State the poll," and people would be waiting to buy the paper.

Number 4 The Mayorhold where I was born, used to be a private house before it was made into a butcher's shop. There were some steps up to the front door which was still there after the shop was in being. Men from Jackson's Lodging House on the opposite side of the Mayorhold used to sit on these steps and make a bit of a mess one way or another. So my grandfather fixed a hose pipe to the tap and let water trickle under the door, and so kept the steps constantly wet. This proved to be a very successful way of keeping them off the steps.

My grandfather was the slaughterman for E. Pitts at 4 The Mayorhold. The slaughterhouse used to be up the yard there. In 1929 the Humane Killer became law (ie. using a gun rather than a poleaxe). He did not like it at all, he said no good would come of it and so he carried on using the poleaxe. His fears were proved correct in August that year when Mr Pitts shot his wife, son and himself in their house up Barrack Road, opposite their other shop.

When the furniture and effects were being taken to the Destructor in Bath Street, my grandfather had to have a police escort (on foot of course), as the people down that area were not inclined to see such good stuff go up in smoke.

I think it quite an achievement for my grandfather to have worked on the same job for 54 years.

Christmas 1925, my father became unemployed like a lot more people. He went to collect his holiday money from work and because the foreman realised he had had a drink, he got the sack. It didn't need much of excuse in those days, so like a good many more, he was on the dole, and finding another job was very hard. So he had to go chopping firewood at the then known workhouse (St. Edmunds Hospital) for a five shillings (25p now) grocery voucher. Cigarettes were not allowed from this voucher so you went where you got the most for your five shillings. This brought into being cheaper grocery shops known as Kays. Their slogan being: 'Kays ways pays'.

It was a bit of a vicious circle. If you failed to chop sticks, you lost your voucher. At the same time you were accused by the Unemployment Exchange of not going and looking for work.

In 1927, my father was taken ill with a stroke and so was not able to work. Those days, when anyone was ill, whatever it may be (except broken bones), you had to be indoors by 9 pm in the summer and 7 pm in the winter. If not, you lost any benefits that you were receiving.

When my father died in 1930, my mother drew the princely sum of fifteen shillings (75p) Widows Pension; ten shillings for herself, five shillings for me, nothing for my brother because he was not old enough. But we did get another three shillings when he was 5 in 1931.

My mother, like many more people at that time, still had her pride, and had to be persuaded to go and meet the Board of Guardians, where a certain Mr Hafford reigned supreme. A few days after the meeting, there was a knock on the door and before anyone could answer it, the front door opened, a man half entered, his finger pointed to the far wall and he said "Sell that." That, being the clock hanging on the wall, which was a wedding present from my father to my mother. This happened before we even knew he was from the Guardians. So he got short shrift. Needless to say, we received no extra finance either.

But we did get Father Christmas call in a van. And I remember being given a shoe box containing an apple, orange, some nuts, a new penny and a wind-up racing car.

As I have mentioned before, we were not the only family by far, in this position at the time.

Although work and money were scarce, people did used to help one another when things got really tough. And they used to make the best of things. Like, I remember Bonham's brakes being loaded with people and a barrel of beer and off they would go to Towcester Races or a nutting party. I never did see any nuts when they got back.

Most Saturday nights, there would be a very musical and entertaining evening in the upstairs room at the Green Dragon at the corner of Bearward Street. The landlord being Dickens, whose family were well known in the entertainment business.

Sunday afternoons there was always a game of 'pitch and toss' on the Mayorhold, in front of the Mission, until the Police came walking down Bearward Street and then it very smartly dispersed.

November 5th, 1930, was the night that Finnegan's woodyard went up in flames, caused by a firework. This resulted in quite a bit of excitement in the area around Broad Street.

CHAPTER 2 – 'GRAMMAR BY GASLIGHT'
– Schooldays

Widespread opportunities for literacy and education have only existed within the span of living memory. Lucy Starmer – who followed her mother – as Postmistress at Grafton Street Post Office remembers:

> When Old Age Pensions first came in in 1909, hardly anybody could write their name! My father, when he come out of his office at the end of the day had to witness all these crosses. 'Cause Mum couldn't. Them days they wouldn't let them. I think they do now. But Pa just had to put 'George Starmer' as witness to the crosses. They couldn't write. That happened every week. I used to have a little stack of them.

One of the most fondly remembered schools in the Boroughs was Spring Lane School. The school is still there today, but the old buildings were replaced by modern ones in the early '60's.

Spring Lane School – 1964 and 1986

Our earliest reminiscences of Spring Lane School come from four people who began their schooldays there before the First World War.

John Stevens: I went to Spring Lane School at the age of 3. (1904). I remember the headmistress's name – Old Mother Naylor. She lived in the bottom house in York Road.

I enjoyed my schooldays. I had nothing to complain about. In those days you went by standards but if you didn't get to the standard you stayed down a year 'til you did, you see. So half of our boys used to leave school in Standard Three. That was as far as they got, and as far as some of them wanted to get. And (some) have done very well since, mind you.

I went through to the end of the school year. This was the time when school leaving parted from 13 years of age to 14 years of age and there was a period when you were allowed to take what they called the Labour Examination. If you passed this examination you could leave school. I was 13 in November 1914. I passed this examination in the July of 1914. There was a possibility that passing this examination might gain me an entrance to the Grammar School. So I went back to school, after the holidays. And the War had been declared on 4th August, you see. My father discovered that there was no call for his labour and he was doing 13 hours a week. Couldn't live on that, so I had to leave school.

Kate Wills: What sort of games did you play at school?

JS: Very little. It amuses me to hear about children going on the continent,

all over the place, today, from school. We had, in the years that I was at school, one outing and that was to Pettit's Tannery at the bottom of the street. (Laughter).

KW: Did you have anybody come round to school to check your health at all?

JS: I can't remember any of that. I don't think any of that happened to us. The only people we used to see was either old Butterfield or Campion at Christmas. Butterfield was the editor in charge of the Chronicle and Campion was the editor in charge of the Echo. They used to come round and give speeches to the kids at Christmas. Tell them what good boys they'd been and give them an orange and a few sweets. A bit of cake perhaps.

KW: You mentioned the fact that you knew the names of your school masters, you couldn't name them could you?

JS: The first school master of Spring Lane when I went there was a man named Smith. This would be 1904/5 and he was still headmaster when I went into the big school so that would be when I was 6. Then he retired and his place was taken by Mr Bradley. He came to us from Vernon Terrace.

The teachers then were Fareham, Smith, Kent, Marriott, Prior, Bliss, Amos. I can remember that Miss Naylor was the headmistress of the infants school and her assistant was a Miss Sibley. Of course not all teachers were teacher-trained then, you know. They only went on from being monitors to trainee teachers. There's one woman's name I can remember from the Girls' School, a Miss Swales.

John Short first went to Spring Lane School in 1911, at the age of 5.

John Short: I don't remember a lot about the infants. I can only remember the Headmistress' name was Miss Butler. But I remember going up into the Boys' School when I was about 7. One thing that sticks out in my mind was the half holiday we used to get on the last Friday of the month if there'd been good attendance. Friday morning the headmaster used to send down to Bridge Street – Hamilton's shop, they sold boiled sweets – and these two boys used to come back with a bag of boiled sweets each. I don't know even whether there were 2 or 3 pounds in each bag of these sweets and all the pupils used to have one sweet, or if there was some over they might be lucky if they got two.

Richard Foreman: Were the attendance records actually good enough?

JS: Oh yes. Quite often. That was a monthly affair you see.

Punishments. It wasn't very often that a boy was sent to the headmaster to be punished, but when a teacher sent a boy to the headmaster, he received his punishment and it went into a punishment book. I understand those punishment books are still in existence.

RF: How strict would you say the teachers were?

JS: Some were more strict than others, but I think the teachers that were more strict gave less punishment than the others. When they did use the cane they were pretty hot with it. I don't know what happened in the headmaster's room when they went in there. I think they had to bend over the desk to receive the punishment, so you can imagine what went on. How many times they were beaten I don't know.

RF: The teachers would also use canes in the classroom?

JS: Oh yes.

RF: It would have to be a particularly bad misdemeanor to go to the headmaster?

JS: That's right. Some boys used to cry and some used to have three on each hand and not shed a tear at all. I should say a good many went through the school without having the – we used to say: having the stick. But it was a cane you know. Not like a garden cane, it was a real cane.

RF: Were there other kinds of punishments as well?

JS: Yes. It was before my time – when you went into the boys' school, you went into a lobby and on the wall were rows and rows of dumbells. Wooden dumbells. They started at the bottom – big ones. There was about six rows and when you got to the top they were lighter. So I should imagine that younger boys would have to carry the lighter dumbells. They were given out usually for coming late to school and they used to have to parade up – we called it the 'channel' – up the side of the school, with the dumbells held above their heads. I never saw any boys having that punishment, but that's what they were there for. Heavy, they were ever so heavy. The big ones at the bottom must have weighed about two pounds each. And for young boys to hold up like that. There was a master over them to see that he didn't drop them and, as I say, he'd get a cut across the bottom with a cane.

Singing lessons. That's one lesson I used to enjoy. We had a Welshman come, whilst I was at school to take singing lessons in particular, but other lessons besides. And his name was Mr. Harries. One afternoon he got into trouble with one of the pupils in my class and he received a good thump in the ear. He was a big boy this lad. I won't mention his name. It resulted in him leaving the school anyway. He was a nice chap.

Then we had drawing and painting. That was with Mr. Marriott...Joey Marriott. He was particularly good at drawing and painting.

RF: Can you remember what kind of materials you had to use?

JS: Oh, we had tubes of paint. And in drawing, we could draw anything, you see, a steam engine, a motor car, or anything we fancied. The one year we made a Shakespearean village in cardboard, the church and the houses and farmhouse and animals and all that sort of thing. And painted them. I believe that went out on exhibition in the town hall.

Then we used to go to woodwork to learn carpentry, but we had to go to Campbell Square School to learn that. They'd got the woodwork room there you see. I went for two years and all the woodwork I do now – I'm fond of a bit of carpentry – I learnt there at school. I remember, we used to have to walk up to Campbell Square from Spring Lane. We was walking up Sheep Street and one of the boys got knocked over in the street, I think we were playing football. Can you imagine people playing football in Sheep Street now? Anyway, he got knocked down and he lost his arm.

RF: What was he knocked down by?

JS: I don't know. I believe it was a tramcar.

Also at school, in the arithmetic lessons, we did fractions and decimals. And when decimalisation came along, in 1971, it was no trouble to me. I knew it. Although I'd never done decimals since I was at school.

Another thing about school: we had a school garden. Before we had it, it used to be a coal yard and the boys had to clear this coal yard and dig up bricks and all the rest of it until we come to earth. All the coal dust and bricks were carried away. We had a very nice garden there and that's been useful to me all my life, what I learned at the garden.

Then we played football. We used to go from Spring Lane to Victoria Park, off Spencer Bridge Road, to play football.

Free meals. When I lost my father, I went to the school clinic in St. Katherine's Street for free meals. That was mid-day dinner. But after a time I wouldn't go – but the service was there if anybody wanted to eke out a living by sending the children to have these free meals. They were supplied by the Borough Council. You also went there to have your tooth out or to have your teeth filled. Or your ringworm seeing to. People had ringworm in those days, at school. They also had things in their hair, jumping about...a lot.

At Spring Lane, in the winter – every winter was icy – we had snow and freezing periods every year without missing. And in the winter they (the teachers) used to get buckets of water and throw them down the playground. And the playground sloped,you see, and we had lovely slides in the playground, year after year. Didn't do much good to our boots. Everybody had boots in those days, not shoes.

RF: Would you say that on the whole Spring Lane was quite a happy school?

JS: I should think it was the poorest school in the town, in the poorest district. But I think if you ask the old Spring Lane School boys, they were proud of being a scholar there. The discipline was on the strict side, but we used to like our teachers. There was a boys' school, a girls' school and an infants' school. It was a big school.

RF: Was there ever any crossover between the...

JS: No, never. No mixing at all. They had separate playgrounds. I never did see a girl in our school all the time I was there.

A Spring Lane classroom in 1917. Standing (left) is head teacher Mr. A. Prior (centre) headmaster Mr. H.T. Bradley.

Alf Humphrey started at Spring Lane around the year 1911.

Alf Humphrey: We started about 4 year old. You used to leave at 14 at the time of day. I never moved from Spring Lane School. When it came to the Intermediate (Exam) we'd only got 12 months to go before we left off school, you see. Matter of fact, the teacher said: "It don't matter, you only got 12 months so you needn't pass if you don't want to." None of us passed and we just played football for the school the next year and finished.

It was quite a nice school. Well, I was always happy there. There used to be a passage down right through to Scarletwell Street. (On) one side was a wall with Cumberpatch's orchard the other side. You can imagine what apples Cumberpatch got when there was school kids sat on his wall. He used to come round and complain – of course, we was out the front playing.

Elizabeth Whitney began at Spring Lane in 1912.

Elizabeth Whitney: I went to school when I were 3. At Spring Lane. That was just the usual thing. 3 year olds you went to school at Spring Lane.

We used to have a slate to start with. Then we had copybooks. And then just ordinary times tables and poetry and sums. Just things, just ordinary... not like they learn nowadays. And I left that school at 11. And they opened a school at St. Georges, the Intermediate School. That was the first year they opened it. I went on to Georges when I was 11.

RF: At Spring Lane, what were the teachers like? Were they very strict?

EW: Oh yes. The old-fashioned type. There was one old lady, Miss Mott, they used to call her. We used to hate the sight of Miss Mott. She was strict. Nobody liked Miss Mott.

RF: Going on to St. Georges – what was an 'Intermediate School'?

EW : Well, you had to pass exams and you got to the Intermediate School. They had so many different schools in the area. Like they came from St. James, Kingsthorpe and so many came from there.

We used to do cookery. We used to have to go to Kingsthorpe to do cookery, Kingsthorpe Grove, and it was much higher you see. We was further away from home. We used to play netball there. And it was a better school, like, better education.

RF: And again, was it disciplined?

EW: Oh yes. Years ago, schools were schools. You were frightened of the teachers. I left there. I left school at 14.

The next two speakers first went to Spring Lane in the late 1920's.

Richard Foreman: Can you remember your first day at Spring Lane School?

Reg Tero: No. I can't remember my first day there. I can remember the Zeppelin coming over. The R101 wasn't it? Just before it crashed. I started when I was 4 (1928) so I'd got to be about 6 or 7 when we see the Zeppelin go over.

I can always remember the old leather factory. The factory's still there as a matter of fact. Used to be Wilson and Tilt's leather dressers. A memory that comes back to me was the smell. It was a smell like pear drops. It was the dope they used in the leather dressing and every so often it used to blow off these extractor fans next to the school. At times it would be very strong, when it was extracting. They had a big chimney at the time. I think that's the only memory I've actually got of Spring Lane, there was nothing exciting happened.

I think the most exciting time is when we became 11 years of age and went to Spencer. Which at that time was a fairly modern school. Hadn't been built many years and it was a terrific change to go from the old Spring Lane School with the old anthracite stove up the corner, which you was froze to death sitting at the back. To go into a centrally heated new school with all glass window doors down the sides, looking out onto quadrangles of lawns and a real first class gymnasium. I think this is the part I remember most: the change from the old to the new. Even though I'd got much further to go. I was 11 years of age. You went there from when you was 11 until you was 14. We left school at 14 them days.

RF: Did you have to pass an exam to go to Spencer?

RT: Well, you sat for an Intermediate Exam and that was Campbell Square School. They call it an Intermediate and if you failed that you went to Spencer, so that's how I got at Spencer. There was very few passed in those days, very few. Only a couple of the brightest lads in the class. Campbell Square they used to take them from all round the schools, all round this area and that so... it wouldn't do for all of us to pass. So it was a couple or three from each school that used to manage to get there.

Ron Draper

The Headmistress there was a Miss Freeman. Well, I hated school as a youngster. I can honestly say I never really liked school until my last year at Spring Lane. There was a teacher there, we all had to go past him. He was known affectionately or whatever you like, as Pap Prior. Everybody knew him as Pap Prior. I think I learnt more in 12 months under that man than any other 12 months of school life, until I went to Spencer.

Mrs N. Barnard, Mrs V. Godfrey and Miss Peggy Ward all taught at Spring Lane School, at various time's during the late 1930's and 1940's. The headmaster at that time was Mr Walker, who is remembered with affection by many ex-pupils and teachers. Audrey Walker is his daughter.

Mrs N. Barnard: I always remember that Spring Lane School was, in a sense, a social centre. Mr Walker knew most of the parents. He'd taught them since they were small, and if they came up feeling annoyed he soon said to them: "Now look here, Joe or Jim, I know what you are," and he was able, very quickly, to help them. And that was the spirit about the place. You were helping the children and their parents.

Audrey Walker: I don't know the names of the parties involved but this was my father's luck. (He) always came out on top. He was walloping a boy in the playground – which you could do in those days – and a mother, outside complained. "That's a terrible thing to do, Mr Walker, how could you possibly do that?"

My father said: "Well, wouldn't you like to know why I was doing it, Mrs ---. This boy was being extremely cruel to one of the younger boys." Long pause. "And that younger boy was your son. Now, am I right to wallop him or not?" I said: "Oh, you jammy devil!" And that's always stuck in my mind.

Richard Foreman: What was the general attitude towards discipline in the school?

NB: Well, I didn't see a lot of walloping. Generally speaking, Mr Walker knew them so well that he could manage without. "I'll tell your dad," you know, "Let your dad come up and see me."

Mrs V. Godfrey: It would be the exception, wouldn't it, if he did that?

AW: (Another) thing that sticks in my mind: there was a sort of polite battle going on (with) the factory next door. Father would complain, most politely, about whatever it was they were doing, shoving muck over, and they would apologise profusely and remove it. Then the same thing would happen within the next few weeks. And this went on for years. Sort of amiable bickering.

Miss Peggy Ward: If the wind blew the wrong way, the tannery was dreadful. It was the most appalling smell, all over the area. And the coke stoves... Each classroom had a coke stove, or two. If you were wise, you learned how to make them up, but you had to be very careful, because you'd open the lid to slide some coke in and it'd all flare up. I lost my eyebrows once. They used to smell. One of my chief memories of the area is to do with the smells.

NB: I remember an inspector coming in once. He looked round and he said, rather sarcastically: "Oh, what a lovely view you have from your room." I had to say to him: "Yes, well... These are only appearances. You've got to look a bit deeper."

RF: How do you remember the material state of the school itself?

NB: Well, the building was very poorly built. During the war, my friend and I used to firewatch in a (school) room and, at night, we could hear the rats and mice scurrying around in the stove. And the children were often dirty. I used to tell them to keep back from me when they were reading because I was frightened to death of getting headlice.

PW: It was such an old building. There was a terrific flight of stone steps, it was ever so high. Upstairs, you'd think it was about four flights up, although there was nothing in between, only the headmaster's room and the stock room.

AW: They weren't allowed to run up and down the stairs were they? I always remember going up to that room and – "Boy, what's the rule?"

PW: Yes, on these wide stone staircases you could hear whether anybdoy ran up or down them. Terrible staircase that was. At the top of this flight of stairs there were just two classrooms. It was a funny building.

But the rooms were huge compared with modern rooms, and, by the time I was teaching there, class numbers were not so big. When I went to school there were getting on for 60 in a class, but the numbers were smaller by the time I was teaching. You could do things in those big rooms, couldn't you? You could have your desks in half the room and use the other half for drama, PE and so on.

RF: What sort of numbers had the classes gone down to when you were teaching?

PW: Fortyish. There wouldn't be more. I think 40 was the ceiling.

Mrs V. Godfrey: I believe there was a rule came out that you could have up to 40 in your department, but the infants must be 30.

PW: We'd got lots of empty rooms when I started teaching there. They made an empty classroom into a staffroom. Staffs had never had a room before then. And they joined two together to make a handicraft room.

RF: Why were those rooms empty?

PW: The population had gone down, of course, by then. I started teaching there in '44. Well, you got the rest of the slum clearance after the war.

RF: Can you remember roughly the overall number of pupils in the school at that time?

PW: There were seven classes... probably about 300. Of course it was all very different, because by this time it had become a mixed school. When I went to school there, there was a girls' department, a boys' department and an infants' department. I was at school there from '32 to '35.

RF: In those days, were there special occasions in the school year that you remember?

VG: Well, they had plays at Christmas. They always put on a play in both departments.

PW: I remember there must have been some national celebration, must have been Victory and we had a sort of display in the playground. The Mayor, or someone, came to it. We had one boy to present a buttonhole and we had to borrow things and dress him up because he was... you know, they were poor. A big family of boys.

I remember doing country dancing in the playground, on this occasion, and you couldn't hear the music. It was from a very ancient gramophone, that you used to wind up, and you couldn't hear the music!

RF: Did the school provide dinners?

PW: School dinners weren't eaten at the individual schools, they were eaten at a central place, namely Regent Square Chapel Hall. It was a very high, noisy building. They used to shout at one another. The teachers had to sell them tickets off a roll, at fivepence a go and you had to calculate the money at the end. The teachers used to eat their dinners behind a brick wall that was built at the end of the place. Terrible! Noisy, horrible and you couldn't really control those children because you didn't know them from Adam.

The queue used to reach outside. They just came. They made their own way from their schools and just joined in the queue and that made a noise while they were waiting to come in. They had to wait for places to be empty. Then, I presume, they just walked the streets until school began again. In those days, it didn't begin again until 2 o'clock. We had a two hour dinner break.

MINISTRY OF EDUCATION

L.E.A. Northampton No. 22

School. Northampton, Spring Lane Council School

Regd. No. P.95/22/44

Inspected on 28th and 29th May, 1946
Report by H.M. Inspector.

JUNIOR MIXED DEPARTMENT

The cheerful friendliness of the children, their politeness and general interest in their work are a tribute to the way in which the Head Master and his staff have overcome the influence of drab school premises situated in a depressing part of the town. The success of the social training owes much to the Head Master, who has an intimate knowledge of individual children and their special problems, and his influence extends beyond the confines of the School. He has the loyal support of the staff who willingly co-operate with him.

In the lower part of the School, group reading is proving successful and normal progress is made at each stage, except in the case of a few scholars who have difficulty in mastering the elements of Reading, but these also are responding to the teaching methods employed.

Composition tests written by the higher classes produced some good results and a satisfactory degree of accuracy in sentence construction and spelling by children of normal ability. Efforts to foster oral narration vary throughout the School: Class 4A. spoke with confidence when presenting the plays they had learnt, though it is evident that weakness in articulation has still to be over-come.

The remainder of this chapter deals with other schools in and around the area.

Irene Swainsbury: A lot of schools would be what we called 'Church School'. I mean, I went to St. Katherine's school. That closed and I had to go to St. Andrews School – because that was another church school. Then that closed, and I finished up at Spring Lane. But then, after that, we moved to Kingsthorpe and I finished up in another church school. So, nearly all my childhood was spent in church schools.

Going to church school, we used to have to go to church parade on certain days and – I didn't think of it at the time but I have thought of it since – I think that you missed out a lot on school. We was always having to go to church. Then we'd come out and come back to school and they would send us home because it happened to be a church day. At the time, we used to think – oh, it was lovely. Because we were at home and the kids was all at school. But looking back, when I met up with those children, I always felt different somehow and I think it was the fact that I had missed quite a bit of schooling, because of the days that we used to have off.

Josephine Kent: Funny you should say that because when I went to Spencer School, after we sat our Eleven Plus, I always had trouble with my legs. Because we used to have to walk to school – there were no buses – and it was a long way over to Spencer, they transferred me to All Saints School, down Horseshoe Street. When they sat and assessed what I'd done, I was far in advance than the other children there. When I returned to Spencer School – when this trouble with my legs had cleared up – I was behind. So I can well believe you saying that.

IS: I don't think the education in a church school was as good as some of the others, quite honestly.

Elsie Bull began her schooldays before the First World War at St Katherine's Church of England School.

Elsie Bull: Mr Stevens was the headmaster and we had a very good education. We used to start with Bible Class in the morning. We used to start hymn singing every morning and then we used to go back to the scripture lessons. He'd take parts of the Bible. We used to have arithmetic and then we used to have drill.

Angela Connor: What was 'drill'?

EB: You know – exercise in the playground and all that. Knees up and bend. But we wouldn't be doing somersaults or anything like they do now. We used to play rounders in the playground. By the way, we had separate playgrounds, not mixed. Mixed class, but not playground. And the boys used to play cricket and football and we used to have rounders. We didn't have long in the playground, only about 20 minutes. The bell would go and we'd get back into school. It was 12 o'clock to dinner then go back at 2 'til 4. In the afternoons we'd have sewing lessons. Sort of needlework.

AC: Were you any good at needlework?

EB: No. I couldn't change my needles.

Edna Brown

Edna Brown: I started off at St. George's Primary School when I was 5 (1922), but I should think by the time I really got going I must have been about 5½, because I was off with whooping cough for quite a while. As for the school itself, I don't remember much – only that there was a sort of classroom-cum-hall and, after the mid-day break, there was little green mattresses and we used to have to lie on them for about half an hour. If we didn't go to sleep we had to stay ever so quiet. We weren't allowed to talk.

Pat Edwards: What was the standard of discipline?

EB: Extremely good.

PE: What about punishment?

EB: Oh, we had the cane. I had the cane quite a lot for talking or laughing. You weren't allowed to talk or laugh.

PE: What about prizes or incentives?

EB: We always had a prize day. Right up until I was 14 I'd got boxes of books that I'd had as prizes all the way through schools.

Len Riley

Len Riley: I went to St. Andrews when I was 3 (1907) and I left there the day I was 14. St. Andrews was a church school.

Kate Wills: Do you remember your first day at school?

LR: Yes, well mostly what I remember was the teacher, Miss Hodge, during mid-morning and mid-afternoon, she made us go to sleep and I didn't like that. They was little tiny desks and you put your head on your arm and they expected you to go to sleep. But I was never used to that so I never bothered.

KW: What sort of things did you do at school?

LR: The same things you do at school nowadays. It was a church school and they taught us church readings, Bible readings – every day you'd got that. You reached the top standard, Standard 7 they used to call it, when you was about 11 and you stayed there for about 3 years as I did. You had the same curriculum year after year.

John Stevens is one of the few people we interviewed, who mentions going to evening classes, after he finished school in 1914.

I went to evening continuation classes for three nights a week on Campbell Square for two years. Then I had three years at the Technical College which used to be where the (ABC) Cinema is now. I did fairly well there. In our year nobody completed the third year. You got too much, you see. You were working 54 hours a week. Food wasn't quite as sustaining during the war. You were then going and doing two hours, three nights a week, bringing homework from it.

In the third year, in our maths class, there were five of us left. In the end the teacher was left with nobody. You just hadn't got the stamina to continue with it really.

Of course, you have to remember Northampton was a boot and shoe manufacturing place then. All the education was geared to the boot trade. The engineering trade was squeezed in, they hadn't got the money for it. For instance, although I worked in a foundry all my life, I was a man well before I knew that cast iron was an alloy. It had constituent parts of silica and phosphorus, and all sorts of things which affected its fluidity and final composition. If I'd been born at the same time in Leeds, I should've had a full understanding of that within my general training. In the area in which I was apprenticed, I was in a fringe area. It hindered me a little bit, but that was because the education system was geared to the shoe trade.

LUCY STARMER'S STORY

Lucy Starmer's childhood, and the rest of her working life, was inextricably linked with the story of Grafton Street Post Office, which was just at the Grafton Street end of Lower Harding Street.

Lucy Starmer: I was born at 51 Lower Harding Street (in 1904).

Richard Foreman: How long did you continue living there?

LS: 56 years. I left. I retired. They closed the Post Office 24th September, 1960.

RF: How long had your parents been there before?

LS: Well, that comes back to my Mum. She was 20. Her brother wanted to get married. Grandma and Mum were keeping house for him. He bought a business at 5 Lower Harding Street for them. That was 1887. And when she went it was an underground kitchen with a baker's oven in it. She tells me she used to cook 100 dinners on a Sunday for a penny a time, but if they brought a lard tin with baked potatoes in, she charged them three ha'pence. While she was there she said there was a field facing them, and they had the fair there once. Well, in that field Cooper Street's been built. I was told by an old lady that that field, the rent from that field was to apprentice poor boys.

I think the next thing'd be, in 1896. At the bottom of Grafton Street and St. Andrews Road, was Goldings Factory, nicknamed 'the skin factory', 'cause they processed rabbit skins. The Goldings asked for a Post Office to be opened in Grafton Street. Those days – this is before 1900 – you just asked. Then they made the rule that Post Offices had to be so many yards apart. But they wasn't then.

The Postmaster got it all arranged and it was to be at the corner of Arundel Street and Grafton Street. It was a grocers shop. It was a Miss --- had it. When it came to it, and the stamp was made and so forth, she wouldn't have it; 'cause she'd got to pay for the letter box and pay a builder to insert it in the wall and buy some letter scales, and have a special drawer made in the counter.

Kate Wills: So the Post Office weren't going to provide...

LS: Oh, they didn't those days you see, and when she found she'd got to provide it, she wouldn't have it.

Now then, this is a bit tricky. At that time, the Parson at St. Andrews and the Curate, didn't see eye to eye. I think that's the best way to put it. My Mother sided with the Curate. When the postmaster was in trouble he went to this Curate and asked if he knew anybody who would take it, and he recommended my Mother. When he came, the Postmaster said: "I should think you'd wanted to get out of this heat." You know – with the oven. It was a Mr. Milton, the Postmaster. My Mother said she wasn't a good enough writer. He just said: "Why won't you take it?" He'd got the stamp made, you see, and so forth. He was in a bit of difficulty. My Mother said: "Well, my writing wouldn't be good enough." And he said: "Let me see. Sign your name here." And she'd signed the form you see. So she had it. But she never grumbled about that or anything.

They said: "You've got to go near Grafton Street, because it's named 'Grafton Street'. I mean, they'd have named it 'Lower Harding Street', if it had been originally there. Where the Post Office was – it was empty at the time. Grandma said: "I'll go and see the landlord." and so forth, and she went and she took it over. It was about October time of 1896. My Mother opened it and became Postmistress. She transferred it to me the April of 1939. She died in '59 and I retired in 1960. And so it was in my family from the beginning (until) it was closed. 63 years I think.

Mum married Pa in 1902, and they did it between them. But they wouldn't let my father be the Postmaster because he was a Friendly Society Secretary. It clashed. Because it had a deposit side to his Society. But they said: "You can still carry on."

RF: Which Friendly Society?

LS: National Deposit. My father started it in the town.

They had a deposit system. You paid so much a month. One and sixpence a month, I think. They took the expenses out and you had so much a month if you were ill. But National Deposit had a deposit section. So much was put on deposit and they paid interest on it. And how much you'd got in your deposit you could carry on several years if you were ill.

I used to hear Pa... He had an office at the back of the Post Office. Anybody, at night, they'd come to the back of the Post Office. He'd see anybody who was interested, and explain it all to them.

RF: Do you have any brothers or sisters?

LS: No, I was an only child. I was only 2 when my father's rheumatism came on and it absolutely crippled him. Just the same as he sat on his stool, you know, his knee set. He always got doctor's cures, but there was no pain killers. When you think of it, you can't believe it now, can you?

KW: We'd got to where your mother's in the Post Office on her own and looking after the shop...

LS: Yes. But she'd got her mother, 85, looking after her. Mind you, pa wasn't crippled at once you know, but it gradually got worse and she looked after him. Grandma died a month after the First World War started. But I can't remember not helping in the shop. And I had to help Mum lift Pa out of chairs and that sort of thing.

KW: And so she worked six days a week.

LS: Yes, she wouldn't serve on a Sunday. But they used to pull her leg. They used to make her serve on a Sunday when she'd got the bakehouse. So she said she was grateful when she got the Post Office and could close on a Sunday.

RF: What are your earliest memories?

LS: I can remember Pa walking. I remember going up to St. Lawrence's Church and I went to walk to the bottom of Grafton Street with him and he left Mum to lock up, and I kept looking back to see if Mum was coming. And he was walking ever so slow then, Pa, with a stick you see.

RF: Can you describe the Post Office?

LS: There was two houses. Pa had them knocked into one for the Post Office, in 1912. And the same time as they were doing that, he had flush lavatories put in downstairs. He didn't have to build the lavatories. That was at the top of the yard, but he had a cistern put in. And then, upstairs, he knocked a wall again, so we could get to the other bedrooms. In 1915, they put me in a bedroom of my own, and I was in the other house. And Ma and Pa were...you know.

RF: How big were the houses? Two-up, two-down?

LS: Yes. There was, like, the shop and then there was a door and a room at the back. They was just the same up above. And an underground kitchen, you see. As I say, the lavatory was at the top of the yard.

He (Pa) was having alterations done until 1929. Then we had the notice to say that they were going to widen Grafton Street. I had a notice in 1959, just before my mother died, to negotiate to buy the property. It was my mother's then. She died about 12 months after. So I came out.

RF: Do you remember places where you might have played as a child?

LS: Well, I had to be in the shop. I met a woman, she said: "I can't remember you as a child." But you see, I was 12 when I was sent to the Convent. Well, I never was able to go out to play with the other girls because I had homework to do.

KW: So you really didn't mix with the other children?

LS: I mixed 'til I went to the Convent. I can tell you one thing. There were some little cottages facing the Post Office – and I sat on a step and a girl taught me to crochet. And we crocheted yokes for our pinafores. It was because the paper shop and tobacconist up Grafton Street put some balls of crochet cotton and steel hooks in the window. I think they were a ha'penny and a penny or something. And everybody, us girls, had a craze for crocheting. And we crocheted three trebles and three chains and we crocheted yokes.

RF: So what age did you start helping out in the Post Office?

LS: Well, (in) 1915, they put me in a bedroom on my own. And I can remember that was a new thing then, eiderdowns. Mum was paying Allowances to the wives of the soldiers – and mothers. She gave me them to put in order and I put them all over my eiderdown. Like all the three and sixpences what the soldiers allowed to the mother, so's the Government put something to it. She sent me up into my bedroom just to put them in order.

RF: Can you remember how old you were when you first went to school?

LS: Yes. The day I was 5. And I fell from top to the bottom of the stairs. 'Cause I had to go up and say goodbye to Grandma. She had a room above the shop. Mum made, like, a bedsitter for her. And I went up to say goodbye. It was a Monday – my birthday that day – and as I came out, I was so excited I fell down, top to the bottom of the stairs. I believe my mother was frantic all morning to see me come back. But I had to go to school all the same.

RF: What school was that?

LS: Georges. And it had just been built. It had been built about a couple of years I think.

I was there 'til I was 12. 1916 I went to the Convent. (Notre Dame, Abington Street). And it was the last term. Pa didn't know anything about terms, so I went the last term of the year. 3rd May I remember it was, 1916.

RF: What age were you when you left the Convent?

LS: 18½, because I wasn't very clever. But Pa was determined. I was there until I was 18. He said you learnt more from 12 to 18, but I don't know whether I did.

RF: Can you remember the outbreak of the First World War?

LS: I remember Pa was visiting a secretary round Banbury way. We sat in a cafe having our lunch and then somebody said: "The Territorials have been recalled from camp". We called at Daventry, on the way back, for a drink. Pa couldn't get out, so either the taximan or a friend went, and when he came back he said: "It's just been reported that the Germans have fired on the British Fleet." I was worried to death. Well, I was 10 you see, when it started.

RF: How did it affect your life?

LS: It affected it a lot, because it was a Post Office and people came in for their allowances. And when (their relatives) were killed, you see...

RF: What about the end of the war?

LS: I can remember being at school when the Armistice was signed. We all came out and waited for the flag to go up. And as I came down Bearward Street from school they came out of the factories there, singing: "The War's ended" , or "The bells are ringing" or something. And they was all rushing out.

The parties weren't 'til the next June when they had street parties. I had to sneak out, sort of thing, to take part...

RF: When you left school, you became an 'official' worker in the Post Office?

LS: Well, I just carried on as usual. What happened was: the notice came, 4 o'clock post. The postman who brought it was a rather nice postman – you know, you had your favourites – and he said: "I'll take you up now, Lucy." He took me up to the clerk, Mr. Hockaday and he signed it and that was that.

KW: Did the Post Office close for lunch?

LS: Not until the First World War. Mum used to open at 8, before, and close at 8 at night. Then it gradually got to 9 o'clock to open. At night it gradually got to 9 o'clock to open. At night it gradually got from 8 to 7 to 6 and now it's half past five isn't it? But it was 6 when I left in 1960. And then we had an hour for dinner.

KW: When did you first have electricity?

LS: We had mantles, you know, gas mantles in the shop. Well, Pa was alive when we had electricity put in. He died in 1936.

KW: Presumably, you never had to bother about security until the very last years?

LS: We always had shutters and they always fixed underneath. We had a pin to put through and pin the shutters. And my mother always had a little linen bag for the safe keys and she always put them under her pillow at night and slept on them.

RF: A lot of housing must have gone down while you were still there.

LS: Yes. Well, you see, it was in about the 1930's when they bought out those up Grafton Street and moved them to Wallace Road and Kingsley way, you know. And then, of course, the war came and it stopped all that. They was getting the people out of the houses the side of us about '35.

But you see, I was there all through the war with them all empty, and they put an ARP hut up. A built one. Not just wooden, a proper built ARP station. They were on duty there of an evening and night.

KW: Presumably, people would come in every day to stock up...

LS: Oh yes, they come... you did have the weekly ones...

KW: Did you make up orders?

LS: Well, I suppose we did. They'd leave the basket and so forth you know. When you'd got a minute and they didn't want to stop. But...used to have them on the counter and you used to put sixpence ha'penny – shilling, and you just reckoned them up like that. We didn't have any calculators.

KW: You didn't have a cash register or anything?

LS: No. The Post Office provided you with ready reckoners but I never used one, not for the insurance stamps. I always worked them out in my head. I couldn't use a calculator now – I should touch the wrong things!

RF: Did you have days of the week which were busy days?

LS: Well, Friday. They'd come out of the factories and call for their grocery and some of them would leave them you see – like at dinner time – and then they'd call as they come out of the factory.

KW: Did you have a half day at all?

LS: Yes, had the half day. And the first time my mother had that half day, Thursday, she came and met me out of school at St. Georges. And she did it for a few weeks after that.

'The lamps all round the bedroom windows. They were oil lamps. They weren't electric, because there was no electric in 1911. A man come two or three times during the Coronation days, and he went up a ladder and lit them at night. Of course they'd gone out by the morning'.

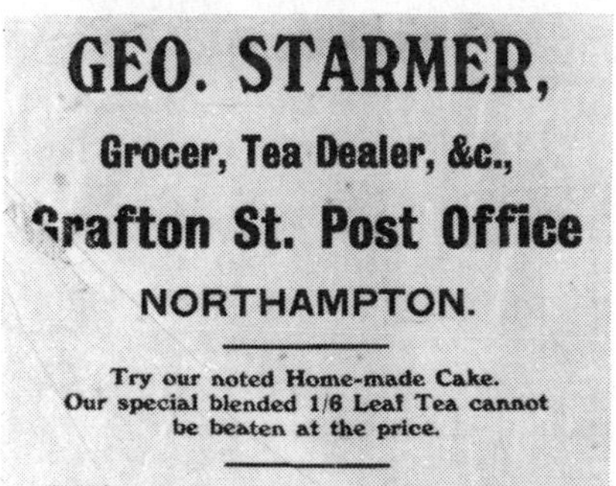

GEO. STARMER,

Grocer, Tea Dealer, &c.,

Grafton St. Post Office

NORTHAMPTON.

Try our noted Home-made Cake.
Our special blended 1/6 Leaf Tea cannot be beaten at the price.

Business Established upwards of Quarter-of-a-Century.

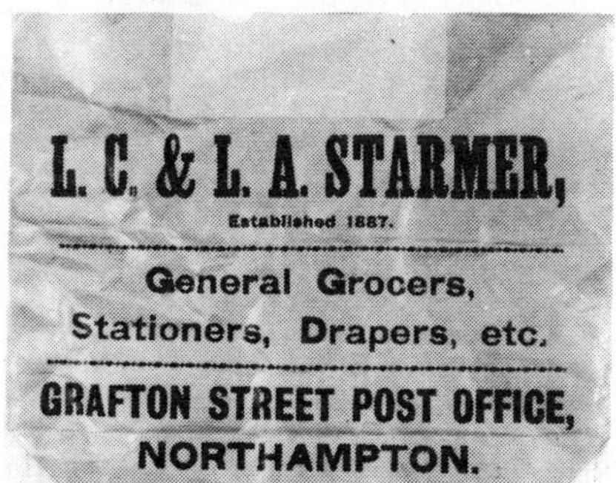

L. C. & L. A. STARMER,

Established 1887.

General Grocers,
Stationers, Drapers, etc.

GRAFTON STREET POST OFFICE,
NORTHAMPTON.

CHAPTER 3 – 'BIG FAMILIES... SMALL HOUSES'

– Housing in the Boroughs

Lucy Starmer

They were bigger families. They were small houses. Johnsons Row – I don't know how they got them in but they did. That was on Grafton Square and you went down some steps and there was a row of houses. I went into one house and you opened the door to go to the back and the wall was just there!

Along Andrews Street there was Union Court, I think it was called, and you went into an opening and there was a row of houses at the back and there was ever such long gardens. And the people living in these houses stood at the top selling the bunches of radishes, you know, what they'd grown in their gardens. I think they all grown their own vegetables but certain ones stood at the top and sold them. I say radishes, lettuces, that sort of thing. Put a little table up, you know.

And there were three courts down Grafton Street. There was a Garden, I can't remember the name. It was lovely in the Autumn. It was all little yellow Chrysanthemums, you know, the little tight buttons. These houses each side... Then there was Kinburn Place and Todd's Lane. There was no gardens there. And they pulled them down and built the Labour Exchange. That was the first thing they did after '29 when we had the notice they were going to widen...

One was very nice at the end of this Gardens. I think the father was a stonemason. His daughter hasn't been dead a couple of years, she was about 90 odd I think. They gave her thirty odd pound for the house when they pulled it down and put her in a house down Scarletwell Street. You know, when they built the flats there. They only paid for the ground it was on. That was at the beginning. Well, I didn't get much in 1960 for mine. I mean, I had to fight for what I did get.

Most of the housing in the area consisted of terraced, two-up two-down dwellings – with some variations, such as basement kitchens. Here, some of these houses are described, beginning with Jim Edwards' family home in Grafton Place. Jim was born in 1924.

Richard Foreman: Can you describe the house?

Jim Edwards: Just traditional. There was a passage in, a front room, living room and kitchen. We'd only got gas lighting downstairs. There was a light in the living room and a light in the front room. You used to have to take a candle to go to bed. And we had a paraffin lamp in the kitchen. There was a big brick-built copper where my mother used to do the washing every Monday. She used to take in washing as well to help out. We used to get the coal up from the cellar on a Monday morning and light the fire. Fill up the copper with a bowl – we only had a single tap in the kitchen. We used to keep chucking the coal on and then that used to take an hour or more to boil. She'd be washing all day long until, oh, ten o'clock at night. And it'd still be there the next day, if the weather was bad and she couldn't dry the clothes. There was no other way of drying them outside.

Inside the living room... the fireplace. 'Grate' we used to call it. One side was a boiler black leaded, and the other side was an oven. So you could boil water one side and the other side you could put something to cook. We had a gas stove in the kitchen, an old black one. Just a couple of burners and an oven. They was quite small and that's why you used to your dinner down to the bakehouse. If there was a big family, you see, the oven wasn't big enough.

RF: Later on when you came out of the army in 1947, did you go back to live with your family?

JE: Well, my father had died during the war and my sisters had married. I went back to live with her. Still in Grafton Place.

Pat Edwards: She lived there 'til the 1960's. By that time she'd got electric light. But the kitchen was very primitive and the toilet was still at the end of the garden with no cistern or anything. You just had to take buckets of water. Even in the cold, icy weather, you still had to go up the garden in the night. And if I remember right, it was a brick path, very uneven, so on the ice it would have been very dangerous. Carrying your bucket of water to throw down afterwards (chuckles). There was no hot water in the kitchen...

JE: When it was wintertime it was just this old paraffin lamp. Which didn't give much light and, oh, terrible it was.

Ron Draper recalls his family home in Bath Square.

Two bedrooms, but one was only really a boxroom, and there was no gaslight upstairs at all. We had candles and for the first part of my life there was only one tap between 12 houses. We used to have to go outside and they used to freeze up in the winter. People used to have burners and candles to defrost the tap so you could get water.

I also remember the time our rents were five shillings and tenpence, rent and rates, and through some Act of Parliament or something, the landlord was forced to put these old stone sinks in. Consequently our rent went up from five shillings and tenpence to six shillings and fivepence per week. This was a fantastic rise to my mother, my father was out of work at the time, and to find that other money was terrible.

When John Short's family moved from Little Cross Street to Fort Street, there was one distinct improvement.

John Short: . . . the Fort Street house had got a built on kitchen, I think made a bit of difference. Kitchen was very small. We had a black gas stove and an old iron mangle and we had a copper up the corner which you heated by the fire underneath It had a chimney going up out of the kitchen. That was for doing the weekly wash. I remember taking that mangle to pieces when I was about 8 or 9 years old! It must have been after my dad died. I was perhaps 10. And a kitchen sink with a tap over. That's all there was in the kitchen.

Richard Foreman: How did you, your three sisters and your Mum and Dad all fit in to such a small house?

JS: Well, I was very young then and I may have slept with my youngest sister. Not quite certain. I know there was two beds in the back bedroom. And of course my Mum and Dad slept in the front bedroom.

RF: What about bathing and toilet facilities?

JS: We used an old – well, it wasn't that old – zinc bath, that we used to do the washing in. Everyone had a bath to do their washing in. They had it in the kitchen sink you see, and what bathing there was done in the bath.

RF: So it was a sort of all purpose water container?

JS: (Laughs) Yes. Well, people's possessions in those days were not very much, you know. I used to have a friend that lived at the top of the street and in his house, in the living room, it was crammed full. They'd got two sisters and two brothers and a mother and father. They lived in a two bedroomed house and in the living room there was a piano and a sofa, a table and about six chairs. And I can tell you it was a job to walk round the table! It could only be about 8 foot by 10, something like that.

RF: What kind of furnishings did you have in your house?

JS: We had a sofa, a table and chairs. Armchair which my Dad used. And that's all. One side of the fireplace there was a cupboard right to the ceiling and the other side there was one about half way up and an open top. You know, like a sideboard on top of the cupboard. Built in. And nothing else in the living room. Pictures and a clock.

Reg Tero, born in Scarletwell Street, remembers the lighting.

And then of course, in those days it was the old candles. You only had gas light in one room, that was the living room. Just the one gas mantle bracket. It wasn't until we moved from there to Horsemarket the first electricity was starting to be put in the houses. I always remember it was £1 a point. £1 for each room. And we had it put in four rooms and in the staircase – £5. It was a wonderful thing then to be able to put a switch down. People don't realise it now. After the old candles and the gas jet going up and down every time you open the door. It was wonderful to put in clean electric.

John Stevens recalls his childhood home.

You know that Crispin Street is halfway down Scarletwell Street and the ground falls away. The door was two steps up from the pavement. The room you went into was the room we lived in. The backroom was a place where everything was done. Now, downstairs, there was a cellar underneath the front room and the kitchen underneath the backroom, you see. Then you went up a wiggly stair. There were two bedrooms up there but there was sort of half-room part way up the stair in which some of my younger sisters slept.

Richard Foreman: Can you remember the furnishing in the house?

John Stevens: Well – deal table and I know the cat always used to scratch one leg. Just the one leg. It was almost cut halfway through with its claws. Windsor chairs and a wicker cradle which I always had to rock because they were all younger than me and I used to rock that and read, you see.

RF: Can you remember what was in the kitchen?

JS: Yes. I can remember this sort of thing. That my mother always had to do her washing in the bath. She had to scrub with a scrubbing board.

Kate Wills: Did she have a mangle?

Broad Street, 1966.

Cooper Street, 1969.

Fitzroy Street, 1961.

At the back of
Grafton Place

King Street, 1947.

Fort Street, 1957.

JS: She did have a hand mangle, a large one with wooden rollers.

RF: So there would be just the one water tap in the kitchen?

JS: Strangely enough, we had one water tap between the four houses outside. But my father was a bit of an individualist, had a plumber put a tap in the cellar you see. So that on one wall of the cellar there was a tap. My mother didn't have to go outside to get water. That was the only difference it made. We had two toilets between the four houses The toilet we used was at the far end and old S-- was a bit of a drunkard so it wasn't always very nice. But that's how it was.

Len Riley was born and spent his childhood in Herbert Street.

KW: How did you get eight people into a small house?

Len Riley: A two-up-two-down. Oh, we fitted in. I've known some sleep head to foot. Like sardines. Parents had one (bedroom) and the others all had to mess in in one bedroom. Sleep how and where you could.

KW: We've heard that people kept rabbits and fowls in their back gardens.

LR: Oh yes. What small garden you'd got. Wasn't so big as this (room). At the bottom of Herbert Street they'd got gardens smaller than this. And don't forget that had got to include the outside loo. (And) hanging out washing – just one sheet and they'd take the lot. In Union Court the gardens were in front of the houses and there used to be a hand pump just on the corner. Now all those people had to rely on the water from there.

Some houses in the area were larger, but this did not always mean that conditions were better. Irene Swainsbury recalls her home.

We lived at number 5 Bull Head Lane. There was four bedrooms, two flights of stairs. We lived with my grandmother. My mother had three rooms there. We just had the one room downstairs. An old, black cooker in there, up the corner. We had a scrubbed, wooden-top table and there was always a clean white tablecloth on it.

We lived right at the top of the house. I didn't used to like have candles to go to bed with. (Downstairs) it was only gas lamps, round the walls. Underneath us there was two big rooms. At one time we had an auntie living down there. They were rooms, they weren't like cellars. As you went out to the back garden there were stone steps on the left hand side, going down to these rooms at the bottom. The toilet was at the top of the garden. There used to be, perhaps, a couple of chickens the other side, in an old pen.

My father always said that there were tunnels under that house went under the Cross Keys and right through to the market square. Right up until he died, which was only about 6 years ago, he said those tunnels were still there. They came all under Sheep Street. He used to say they blocked them up.

Julia Bush: It was a very big house Did it belong to your family?

IS: It must have been rented.

JB: But it was all members of your family living there?

IS: Yes. My grandmother, three uncles lived there, then two of them got married. I can remember at nights the men used to sit on the doorstep, out the front, with a bit of bread and cheese and perhaps a pint of beer.

We moved because of the overcrowding. We'd only got two bedrooms. Mother and Father was in one. My two brothers were in a double bed and I was in a single bed in the same bedroom. (So) it was classed as overcrowding.

Joyce Hall was born in King Street and spent her childhood in number 21 which was attached to the yard of her father's firm, Walker and Cooke, cabinet makers and wheelwrights.

It was a large house in a very narrow street. On the corner, from Horsemarket there was a pub and we were next door. We took up a tremendous amount of the street. There were about another three little houses next to ours.

We had this underground kitchen where we all had our meals and a back scullery. A stone-floored scullery with a copper up the corner that we had to stoke up and fill Friday nights when we had a bath. (We) had a zinc bath on the floor, took it in turns (and) shut ourselves in. A coal place that was over-run with mice. We had to have cats to keep those down. Then there were stone steps up into the yard. Above that was a nice, big sitting room (in) which we used to try and have meals, weekends. We used to go up and down and fetch everything from below because there was no running water on that floor at all. Behind that was a front room and then there were bedrooms. No bathroom, just four bedrooms. So Mother and Father had one and we children had one each.

CHAPTER 4 – A SHOP ON EVERY CORNER'
– Food and shops remembered

A look through any Kelly's Northampton Directory for the first few decades of this century will confirm the memories most people have of the great number of small shops in the area. And yet, as one person commented, 'they all seemed to do a trade. They never went bankrupt, like they do these days.'

Most of the people we interviewed enjoyed at least one mental wander down those old streets, recalling the names of shops, pubs and their proprietors.

John Stevens: At the corner of Bell Barn Street and Grafton Street was Abrahams a pawn brokers and further up there was a fellow who used to specialise in all sorts of bicycles, riding bicycles until quite recently, I think...

Kate Wills: Mr. Higginson.

JS: That's right. Then there was a newspaper shop, then was a barbers' shop and, just above St. Andrew's Street which came out opposite Tees the bakers, was the Roebuck. Just beyond there was Letts, who used to sell upper leather and bottom leather for people who used to make shoes.

Ann Bonham... used to be on the Mayorhold and next to the Jolly Smokers was her jobbing yard where she kept her horses. She used to run a service for the Post Office. In those days the Post Office hadn't any transport of its own. Ann Bonham used to do all that. Fetch the post from the station to the Post Office for sorting; then take it out to the villages.

KW: There seemed to be quite a few sweet shops in the Boroughs.

JS: Oh yes. Well, there was this little one straight opposite Scarletwell Street; Perrins on the Mayorhold; Motts at the bottom of Cooper Street.

KW: Was this the Mrs. Mott who used to cook toffee?

JS: All sorts of things were home-made stuff. I remember Fry's chocolate bars. Anticipation. Realisation. Expectation...(laughs). One of the first advertisements I remember was: 'The ghost of tabby, fed on skim, was all there were a'left of him Then it went on to tell you about the fat old one that had been fed on Nestles.

On the market square they used to sell boiled sweets. Boiled sweets were the big thing. Loose. Fishes and orange quarters and all that sort of thing. From all of this, shovelling them up, there was always little bits chipped off. In the end they used to gather that up and called it waste. We used to buy a ha'porth or a farthing's worth of waste and take it to school with us.

Almost everyone remembers the bakehouses.

Jim Edwards: When I was a lad there was (a bakery) at the bottom of the street. Used to do all the dinners on Sundays. I think it was tuppence to take your dinner to be cooked. It wasn't just your Yorkshire, everyone seemed to have a joint of meat of some description. You had your name stuck in the top and (the baker) used to put it in the oven with a long sort of paddle – like an oar, although flat. He used to push it right in. When you used to go and get your (dinner) he used to slide this paddle in and bring it out again. There was your dinner cooked. Quite hot. You always used to take a couple of bits of cloth to carry it with and a nice clean tea towel to put over the top.

The old gas stove just wasn't big enough to put a Yorkshire in.

Elizabeth Whitney: Our mother used to have a tin like that. You used to have a Yorkshire, and then in the week you took baked potatoes. There were no messing about. You had a joint. You had half a leg of lamb. You didn't have messing about bits.

You'd fetch it (from the bakehouse) at a certain time. You'd see everybody with a towel holding the tin coming back. Everyone did, because the old cookers, they weren't like they are now. I mean, you just lit up. You lit your kettle, in the oven. You couldn't cook like that. (At the bakehouse) it was a great big oven. A fire underneath. It wasn't gas.

Josephine Kent and Irene Swainsbury fill in the picture a little more and go on to consider other aspects of shopping and eating.

Irene Swainsbury: On Sundays they never used to cook their Yorkshire puddings in the house. They used to take them to the bakehouse in Scarletwell Street. There used to be perhaps two or three of the women, get the Yorkshire pudding in the tin with the meat, put a cloth over it, walk down to the bakehouse and, while that was cooking, they'd go in the pub and perhaps have a couple of glasses of stout. Then they'd go back to the bakehouse, pick the dinner up and bring it home to be dished up in the house.

Josephine Kent: It used to be thruppence for a small tin and sixpence for a big tin. Used to be Jeffery's, the bakers down Scarletwell Street. The

Crispin pub used to be next door. I can remember people going in Jeffery's and saying: "I want it well done," and "Don't burn my pudding this week," and this sort of thing. According to how you wanted it cooked that's how he placed it in the back. If it wasn't to be too well done it would be in the front.

IS: I can never ever remember anybody dropping one.

JK: I can. I can remember when I was little, coming up... It was this tray of baked potatoes and it belonged to a lady in Scarletwell Street. She dropped it and the potatoes went on the floor. She picked them up, put them back in the tin and carried on home.

IS: I think this baked potatoes is something for Northamptonshire. It's an old dish. They used to put pastry round the tin, put all the potatoes in, sprinkle a bit of gravy salt and put the meat in the centre. We always had that on Wednesday.

Julia Bush: Not on a Sunday?

IS: No. On a Wednesday.

JK: Always had Yorkshire pudding on a Sunday. Always.

JB: What meat did you have?

IS/JK: Beef.

JK: I used to go to the butcher's every Monday morning, before I went to school. Kings, down Marefair. Mondays, we'd have the leftovers from Sunday; Tuesday, you'd have two penn'orth of stewing meat and a penn'orth of liver. Then on Wednesday we always had a bit of beef to bake, sixpence. You always told them how much you wanted to pay and they'd cut you a little piece of beef. So we used to have Yorkshire pudding Wednesdays and Sundays. On Thursday, most probably, a liver and onion roll or a bacon and onion roll. It was filling. Used to have plain roll with treacle on...

JB: Did you have one day when you'd do a big shop?

JK: Well, my mother always used to go to the Home and Colonial in the Drapery. We used to go there Fridays and get the groceries. I can remember them always tying it up into a brown paper parcel with string round. Always had your grocery wrapped for you.

IS: And the butter used to be in a big pat. I can see the man now with two bits of wood, patting it.

JK: Then putting a pattern on top.

IS: Then just weighing it onto greaseproof paper. And then they used to wrap it up.

They used to have pigs' trotters and pigs' tails. My father always used to say the only waste on a pig was the squeal! They used to have pigs' heads. One part of it they used to make into brawn and the other part they'd perhaps roast with the baked potatoes, or something like that.

Bob Stanton writes of his own memories of family meals.

Bread and lard was eaten a lot by most families, daily. It was taken to work quite a bit for lunch.

Yorkshire pudding was a very popular Sunday lunchtime meal, with or without meat. As also was baked potatoes with a crust round. Fish and chips costing thruppence; fish tuppence, chips a penny. And if you asked, they would always give you some batter bits to go with your chips.

Stew was always good. Everything was put in an earthenware stew jar, put in the oven at the side of the fire and just left. There would be stewing meat, dumplings and gravy. When it was ready, it was a meal to relish.

Stewed eels and mash from Hodges up Bearward Street was another favourite supper.

Reg Tero adds:

I think the main food at tea time was jam. We always had pots of jam. A lot of women in those days used to make a lot of home made jam and, spread on a piece of good, old thick bread, that was as good as a meal. In fact a lot of them down there, probably, that's all they did have for a meal at times. Because bread was cheap.

We never had anything out of the ordinary. We only used to have a sweet on a Sunday, not every day. Then, we may get rice, or even go as far as a tin of pineapple chunks. Pineapple chunks in them days was the cheapest fruit you could buy, much cheaper than peaches or pears or anything like that. So it was only on a Sunday we had a real sweet after the meal.

John Short's memories of a Boroughs diet also include the First World War:

I don't know how my mother managed it but we always had enough to eat. But the quality of what we had wouldn't be acceptable to anybody today. Not to anybody. Not the poorest would live on those kind of things.

During the war we had margarine and it was different to what the margarine is today. From the Maypole. A firm called Maypole. And that got short and...instead of margarine we got coconut butter. And it was... you know, if you have dripping in a pan or in a basin, you can tip it out in one piece. And coconut butter – when you went to cut it, it used to fly in all directions. It was brittle. And it was the devil to spread.

I remember eating and enjoying cods' heads. They were lovely. In cods' heads – I know this because I was in the fish trade all my life – there's two little bits of ivory. About as big as your thumbnail and a bit longer and a bit narrower. They were a bit bent and on the underneath side they were serrated. We used to get these little bits and play with them. But they made a good meal, cods' heads.

There was always plenty of vegetables. You could get a penn'orth of pot herbs. Which means a carrot, a swede, a turnip... And perhaps an onion if you were lucky. And a bit of meat. They made a stew. My mother used to put all these in a stew jar and we had an oven in the fire-grate. She'd put that in at night. It'd still be warm in the morning. Then she'd finish it off in the gas stove and well, you got a meal for pence. For under a shilling.

Richard Foreman: What meats were available?

John Short: Breast of mutton. In the 30's a bit of meat used to be fourpence. Just before the Second World War. So in the First World War it would perhaps be a bit less than that.

We used to have milt. I used to love milt when I was a kid. I don't know what part of the animal that is. A bullock. You can still buy it for animal food.

Puddings. We used to have a lot of rice and sago. Milk puddings, see. And bacon and onion rolls. Made in a dough. Or Spotted Dick. They were nice too.

I don't remember ever having bacon or egg for breakfast until after I left school. And that was only Sunday mornings.

Pontings pork butchers. You could go there Fridays, Friday afternoons, Friday evenings. You'd get a basinful of faggots or a basinful of chitterlings. Insides. They're all the pipes, all cleaned and boiled. They were blooming handsome. They're not half as good now – you can only get frozen ones and they're not the same article. They used to serve them hot, you see, straight from the copper. And the faggots, they were made up from all offal. They were a penny each. You get a basinful of them and there were enough for a family – for about sixpence.

Joyce Hall saw all this from the other side of the counter.

Friday night was a big night (for) my uncle along at the butchers, because they used to make their own faggots. I can remember having to go along and help lift them into the shop. At the side of his main shop he had another window with a passage in and that was the Friday night shop. They had these big tins of faggots, black puddings, pigs' heads – all offal. He used to do all his own cooking at the back as well. Friday night was a big thing when the men came home from work and the wives would run along with their basins and trotters and things like that. Used to have to scoop one portion and put it in their dish.

Born in 1922, in Burwell, Cambridgeshire, Mary Smith came to Northampton in 1931, when her parents took a house in Broad Street. Her father – who had lived in the Boroughs before she was born and had run a grocer's shop in Scarletwell Street – worked in the printing trade. Her mother ran a grocer's shop, Harnwell's on the ground floor of the house. Here, Mrs. Smith talks about her memories of working in the shop as a child.

Mary Smith: I loved it. I think children do, really, especially weighing things up. There was the lodging house opposite. The poor old men used to come in and they'd buy ha'porths and penn'orths of tea and sugar. I used to love making the little cones up with squares of paper for weighing up the tea and the sugar. And then we used to cut up butter and marge in small quantities for them.

Kate Wills: What other sorts of things did you sell in the shop?

MS: All sorts. We used to have a nest of drawers where we had dried lentils split peas, pearl barley and all that sort of thing. We used to weigh them up, mostly in half pounds or quarters.

KW: Did you sell blue bags?

MS: Oh yes, and the old wooden pegs. We'd got quite a big window and I used to love to help set the window out with little dishes with loose sweets on. Dolly Mixtures.

KW: You were saying that chocolates came in big, wooden crates from Lyons.

MS: Bars of chocolate. How many there would be in a box I don't know. Perhaps about two or three dozen. A lot of the sweets came in wooden boxes then.

KW: What would a bar of chocolate have cost?

MS: A bar of Cadbury's chocolate, which is now 10p or 12p, was an old penny and you had little ha'penny ones as well, half that size.

KW: And you sold boiled sweets?

MS: Yes. We had the cheap sweets which were tuppence a quarter and then the better ones – which I used to love – 'egg and milk rolls', they were fourpence a quarter. But, you know, there'd be the old gobstoppers and peardrops.

KW: So the kids came in from school, spent their ha'pennies with you and went away with gobstoppers?

MS: Yes. And little round boxes. I think they were a kind of a thin wooden one which had kali in. A little kind of a spade thing to eat it with. Or the sherbet bags with the bit of liquorice in and a stick thing with a bit of toffee on.

KW: What were your opening hours?

MS: I can't remember really, but we were open quite late in the evening.

KW: Did you get a lot of customers during the day?

MS: Oh yes, quite a lot.

A variety of other shops are remembered in the rest of this chapter – Jim and Pat Edwards

Jim Edwards: Up Grafton Street we had the little alleyways and the Chinese laundry at the top. Leong Ah Yow. Big family of them. They got above (the door) a midday sun with all the rays coming out round it. That was before the Labour Exchange was built.

Pat Edwards: Wasn't it renamed the Sunlight Laundry?

JE: Yes, it was. I can picture that now. Must have been about the time the Labour Exchange was built.

Elizabeth Whitney

Elizabeth Whitney: And then next door was Briody's. She made all home made sweets. It smelt beautiful. She used to make clove rock, home made. The smell used to be lovely as you went by. Home mades, toffee apples... About a penny a quarter. Well, you could get a ha'penny's worth, even a farthing. You could get a farthing's worth of sweets.

Pat Edwards: She used to make ginger beer as well.

Jim Edwards: There was quite a few people made that around here.

Irene Swainsbury and Josephine Kent

Josephine Kent: I can always remember the old pawnshop at the top of Broad Street. They used to queue up there Monday mornings to put things in pawn. Friday night they used to be another queue to fetch them out for the weekend. Women used to put their husbands' suits in on a Monday morning and fetch them out on a Friday night so the men could go out Saturday and Sunday. Used to be a hell of a long queue there.

IS: My Mother always said she'd rather go to the pawnshop than ask anyone to lend her any money. She used to go along on a Monday morning. Used to do the washing and, when it was all washed and ironed, take it down the pawnshop. Then take it out on a Friday, ready for everbody to have their clean clothes on at the weekend.

Julia Bush: This was a regular thing?

JK: Yes.

IS: The pawnshops did well in those days. People used to pawn their wedding rings or their engagement rings. They'd pawn them for a couple of weeks 'til they'd saved up enough money to fetch them out. I'm afraid a lot of people never fetched them out 'cause they couldn't afford them.

JK: No. That's why Osborne had always got some good second hand wedding rings for sale.

The Co-op

Photo courtesy South Midlands Co-op.

The Boroughs area of Northampton is closely linked with the early history of what was to become the South Midlands Co-operative Society. In late 1870, a meeting at the Red Lion, in Horsemarket, led to the establishment of the West End Industrial Co-operative Society. Their first store was opened at 43 Marefair.

At the end of its first quarter of trading – January 21st, 1871 – the dividend paid to members was one shilling and sixpence in the pound. By 1873, depression caused this figure to fall to sixpence. Times had improved by 1878 when it rose to two shillings. Fluctuations continued however. In 1890 there was no dividend at all.

By the turn of the century the Society had sold the Marefair premises and both opened and closed a shop at 24 Castle Street. Bread was baked at a bakehouse in Bell Barn Street. The trade was so good that two more ovens were installed at the rear of Castle Street.

Now there were numerous branches throughout the town and the Northampton Co-operative Society (it was renamed in 1900) was firmly established. In 1978 it merged with Luton to form the South Midlands Co-operative Society.

A TOUR WITH MAX ALLEN

I propose to take you on a tour of one of the oldest parts of Northampton. I refer to Horsemarket, the Mayorhold (pronounced by Northamptonians 'Merald'), and the streets in the vicinity as I personally call to mind over the last 50/60 years.

Horsemarket

Here there were some four to five dilapidated houses which had, at some time or another, been knocked into one and taken by Russell Seal. They were wholesalers to the cycle and motorcycle trade, with spares, electrical accessories tyres etc.

I knew quite a number of the staff there and I readily call to mind the following: Mr. Noel Green, Roger Notton and Mr. Hanock. The whole place was a hive of industry, every room stacked with stock, assistants running up and down stairs fetching this and that for customers. Although the whole place looked chaotic, it must have been organised chaos – because everyone knew where everything was. There appeared to be so many little rooms, it was just like a rabbit warren.

There was a gents' hairdresser by the name of Faulkner; the Red Lion; the Augustine Motor Garage (Cave and Son) and the Northampton Wireless Relay Company. Their offices were nearby in Gold Street. The proprietor was Mr Ray Turner, who opened the Temperance Hall in Newland – one of the oldest silent cinemas in the town.

One must not forget the very tall garage of Grose which had its showrooms and offices at the corner of Pike Lane, off Marefair, running through to the Horsemarket. It was so big one could not possibly miss it. They eventually moved to a more modern showroom in Queen's Park Parade.

I have my own special affection for Grose's Garage, all a result of the following:

As a boy of 11 years plus, I first went out to work at a local sports shop at the end of Abington Street, where I made myself useful. After some two years, the firm went bankrupt. However, another firm took over and decided to keep me on until I was 14 years and left school when I could go full time.

I was very fortunate insofar that this firm employed a young manager and his wife, who lived in a flat above the premises. My face fitted and I very quickly gained their friendship. They took to me and I to them. It was not long before it was the recognised thing for me to spend most weekends at their flat. They would take me out with them in their car on the Sunday.

It became a habit, at about 4.30pm on Saturday afternoon, providing we were not too busy – for me to go down to Grose's, where the car was garaged, to see that she was filled up with petrol and oil, polished and generally ready for our day's outing. There were some dozen or so cars garaged there, including ours. I'll never forget it, it was an 'Albert'. I had not seen one before, and have never seen one since.

I became fascinated with this car and, very soon, learned how and what made it tick. Theoretically, I felt I could drive. All I wanted was the chance to do so.

As the cars were spaced only some couple of yards apart, it gave me little room for maneouvre. It was not long however, before I was moving this car, only – of course – in one gear, forward, right up to the next car, without touching, and reversing, which was a little more difficult. Having done this dozens of times, I was confident that all I needed was the chance to get her on the road and the rest would be easy.

This knowledge stood me in good stead. Later in life, I obtained a job and was told, "A car will be provided and you are to collect same from a certain garage in Kettering."

After locating same, I asked the garage attendant if he would get the car out of the garage, on to the road for me, at the same time dropping five shillings into his hand – worth having in those days. He did, furthermore, I accepted his offer to stay with me for a mile on the road. Then I ran him back to the garage.

Now the road from Kettering to Northampton I considered just what I needed to really get some practice in the handling of this car. I went in speeds, slowly at first, then fast; got to know the gears; stopping and starting, reversing off the road into farm gateways – up to but not touching the actual gate.

I only once reversed – 'bump' – into a gate, but no damage. In the 14 miles I had to practice in, I was now a self-taught driver, and of course, in those days – no driving test! To cut a long story short, I was driving in Birmingham's Bull Ring, of all places, the next day.

Now you can understand my affection for Grose's Garage.

Broad Street

An elderly lady, whom I had the great pleasure to know, lived on Broad Street. This was Mrs. Ann Bonham. One of her sons, a heavily built man, was then proprietor of Ann Bonham and Son, funeral undertakers. He had two sons, Dennis and Cyril, and a daughter. After his death the two sons carried on the family business, which had been established since 1850.

St. Andrew's Street

A Mrs. Howes ran a wet fish shop. I remember her very well. Her bark was worse than her bite. I seem to remember another fish shop run by a Mrs. Allard. Just the opposite type of person to the Mrs. Howes previously mentioned.

Bull Head Lane

This connected Sheep Street to the Mayorhold.

During the time of the Macrea murder in Northampton, there was a taxi driver (pony and trap, of course). The murderer hired him to take him to Chapel Brampton, where later the remains of the female victim were found in bacon sacks. I am informed by his great grand-daughter that the driver lived in a cobbled alley that ran from the Mayorhold to Sheep Street, and I can only conclude this to be Bull Head Lane.

Regent Square

George Westley of the Wheatsheaf Inn was also, I believe, a cabby in the very early days of the motor taxis.

In the near vicinity of Regent Square Methodist Church, a Miss Sarah Manning, an elderly lady, lived with her brother. Once, she gave me a brass jug she knew I had always admired, saying she would rather know I had the pleasure of it whilst she was alive. I still have it and remember her every time I clean it.

Do you remember the drinking fountain in the centre of Regent Square, erected in the memory of a prison governor and subsequently demolished after a car ran into it?

Grafton Street

J.A. House – a pawnbroker and house furnisher, affectionately known as 'Jonah House'. This shop was at the corner of Fitzroy Terrace.

Sheep Street

As a young man it was always exciting to go into the Bear, a very popular pub in this street. Another exciting pub I used to spend an hour or so in was the Ram Hotel. It was run by a Mr. Markham, his wife and his wife's sister, Barbara – she being the life and soul of the evening.

Further along this side of Sheep Street came a very tall building. I rather fancy it had a history. 'Locock's Hill'. The pavement past the house gradually sloped upwards, leading to a level along the width of the whole building and then sloped downwards again. Whether this, at some time or another, was to enable a person to mount a horse by the roadside, I don't know. I can think of no other reason.*

King Street

On the left hand side was St. Katherines Church, which, when later demolished, became the garden of rest. The statue, 'Woman and Fish', was erected in May 1952. It was vandalised and eventually found a new home in Delapre Park.

Bath Street

All I can remember of Bath Street was the premises of Harry Ponting, a dairyman. I remember the fresh-complexioned, grey-haired, elderly lady – hair very untidy, whisping over one side of her face – sitting between what appeared to be huge barn doors and serving milk to anyone who happened to call.

St. Mary's Street

I have only one memory of this street. Whether this was a figment of my imagination, I'll never know. I must have only been a boy of about 7 years. There comes a picture to my mind of a thatched cottage, roses around the door . . . a perfect picture. The occupier dressed as a farm yokel used to dress in an embroidered smock and a deep straw hat. He was clean shaven, apart from a very narrow growth of beard under his chin.

What struck me as strange was the absence of any other house. I wonder if this was intended to be a preserved building, during the clearing of the ground for the building of the flats that eventually came.

Here end my memories of this particular part of town.

Max Allen has written extensively about old Northampton and would be happy to hear from any prospective publisher. He was proprietor of Allen's Sports and Rubber Wear Shop which, for many years, was on the Kettering Road. Mr. Allen is retired, but his son still runs the business – now located in the Grosvenor Centre.

**Jon Small writes: Dr. Henry Locock, Mayor of Northampton in 1749, lived here and had the 'hill' built to enable him to enter his carriage on the level. It was demolished in 1927.*

CHAPTER 5 – 'THEY LIKED A DRINK.'
– Pubs... and the Police

Richard Foreman: When was the Twenty Fives pub knocked down?

Lucy Starmer: Oh, not ever so many years (ago). The landlady, well, her son had it after her. He died, her son. In the First World War it was put out of bounds to soldiers 'cause it wasn't conducted very (well). But the Welcome was always conducted so well. The Lily of the Valley pub, was in Bell Barn Street, just at the end. It went into St. Andrew's Street.

Kate Wills: In Lower Harding Street at the time, you had the pub on one corner next to you...

LS: Then the next was the Welcome which is still there. And the next corner down, not Compton Street but Monks Pond Street, was the Spotted Dog, and then in Francis Street was the Robin Hood. Further along there was a pub again and that was the Earl Spencer Arms. Corner of Compton Street was the Prince of Wales.

Len Riley recalls his childhood impressions of Boroughs pubs:

Len Riley: My father went straight from work into the pub and that was that. I think his (favourite) was the Harding Street Tavern. There was one in Brook Street and another one facing that, called the Chequers. I used to have to go and meet him out of work 'cause he got seven and six – the wages for him then.

(Beer was) only a penny a pint. My mother used to say "Go and meet your Dad out of work and get some money from him." Meet him out of work on Saturday lunchtime and, if I was lucky, I got five bob off of him. And two and six for his spending money, beer and card games. They played for a pint of beer.

A newcomer to Northampton, in the 1930's, Eileen Allard was introduced by her husband to the social life of the Boroughs.

Eileen Allard: . . . That's the first pub he ever took me in. It was ever so strange to me. There was a band in there, (someone) playing the banjo and two more musicians. A man come in with a basket – with a white apron on – selling cockles and mussels and 'hard bits', they called them.

Jim Allard: They were whelks.

Whether they frequented them or not, everyone remembers the pubs of the Boroughs. There were a lot of them. John Small lists the following:

1. Albion
2. Althorp Arms
3. American Banner
4. Bakers' Arms
5. Bakers' Arms (a.k.a. Army and Navy
6. Bath Tavern (Old)
7. Bear (a.k.a. Tavern in the Town)
8. Bee's Wing
9. Bird in Hand
10. Black Lion (Old)
11. Blue Anchor (Old)
12. Blue Bell
13. Boot and Slipper
14. Bricklayers' Arms
15. Broad Street Tavern
16. Bull
17. Bull & Butcher
18. Bull's Head
19. Bunch of Grapes
20. Burghley Arms (a.k.a. Dun Cow & Bearward Arms)
21. Castle (Old)
22. Chequers (Old)
23. Cherry Tree
24. Coopers' Arms
25. County (Hotel)
26. Cream of the Valley
27. Cricketers' Arms
28. Crispin's Arms
29. Criterion (Old Site A.K.A. Sultan & Fountain)
30. Criterion (New Site)
31. Cromwell Arms
32. Cross Keys
33. Earl of Northampton's Arms (a.k.a. Northampton Arms)
34. Earl Spencer's Arms Inn
35. Eclipse
36. Falcon
37. Friendly Arms
38. Gardeners' Arms
39. Gate Inn
40. Globe
41. Golden Lion
42. Grafton Arms
43. Green Dragon
44. Hop Vine (a.k.a. Vine)
45. Horsemarket Tavern (a.k.a. Maltsters Arms)
46. Jolly Bricklayers
47. Jolly Tanner
48. King's Arms
49. King's Head
50. King Street Tavern
51. Lily of the Valley
52. Live and Let Live
53. Mitre
54. Moat Tavern
55. New York Tavern
56. North Western Hotel
57. Oak Inn
58. Old Jolly Smokers
59. Prince of Wales
60. Quart Pot Inn
61. Railway Tavern (Old)
62. Ram
63. Red Lion
64. Rising Sun
65. Rivetters' Arms
66. Roebuck Inn
67. Rose and Punchbowl
68. Saddlers' Arms
69. Sewing Machine
70. Shakespeare (a.k.a. Crow and Horseshoe)
71. Sportsman's Arms (a.k.a. Forget Me Not)
72. Spotted Dog
73. Star
74. True Blue
75. True Blue (Old)
76. Trumpet
77. Twenty Fives (a.k.a British Banner
78. Welcome Inn (a.k.a. Wallace & Hero of Scotland)
79. Wheatsheaf
80. White Horse
81. White Lion
82. Curriers' Arms

a.k.a. - 'Also known as' - ie. some pubs had more than one name over their lifetime.

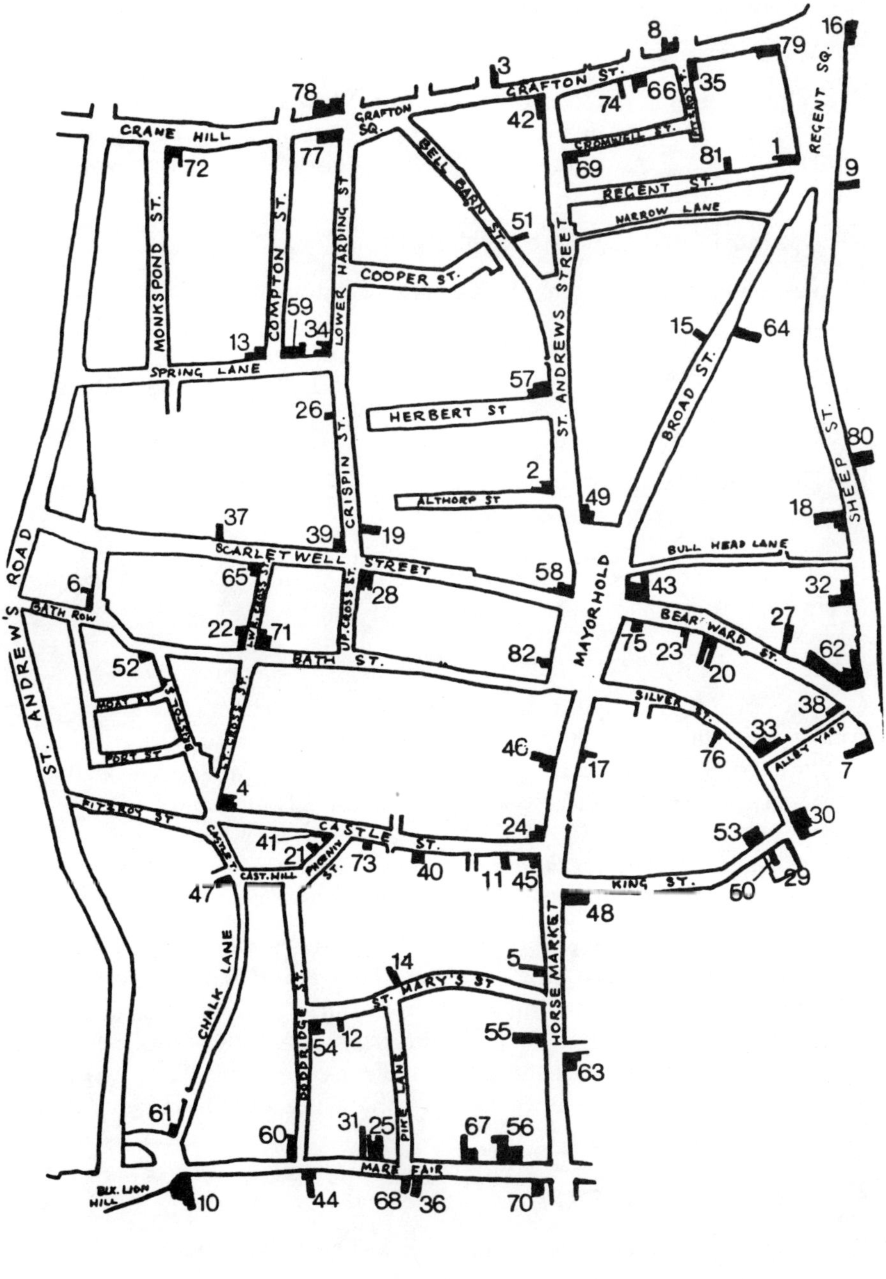
CRANE HILL
GRAFTON SQ.
GRAFTON ST.
CROMWELL ST.
FITZROY
REGENT ST.
REGENT SQ.
NARROW LANE
BELL BARN ST.
COOPER ST.
MONKSPOND ST.
COMPTON ST.
LOWER HARDING ST
SPRING LANE
HERBERT ST
ALTHORP ST
ST. ANDREWS STREET
BROAD ST.
SHEEP ST.
BULL HEAD LANE
CRISPIN ST.
SCARLETWELL STREET
ST. ANDREW'S ROAD
BATH ROW
LWR. CROSS ST.
UP. CROSS ST.
BATH ST.
MAYORHOLD
BEARWARD ST.
SILVER ST.
ALLEY YARD
MOAT ST
BRISTOL ST
PORT ST
LY. CROSS ST.
FITZROY ST
CASTLE ST.
CASTLE ST.
CAST. HILL
PHOENIV ST.
KING ST.
HORSE MARKET
CHALK LANE
DODDRIDGE ST.
ST. MARY'S ST
PIKE LANE
MARE FAIR
BLK. LION HILL
1
2
3
4
5
6
7
8
9
10
11
12
13
14
15
16
17
18
19
20
21
22
23
24
25
26
27
28
29
30
31
32
33
34
35
36
37
38
39
40
41
42
43
44
45
46
47
48
49
50
51
52
53
54
55
56
57
58
59
60
61
62
63
64
65
66
67
68
69
70
71
72
73
74
75
76
77
78
79
80
81
82

EA: I'd never seen anything like it.

Richard Foreman: Which pub was that?

EA: The George and Dragon. In Georges Street. Old Mrs. Miles. (She was) about 70 when (Jim) sold her a donkey. She said, "Here Jim, that donkey's in foal." And (he) said, "Well, better the donkey than you, Mrs Miles!"

RF: Did musicians play there regularly?

JA: Yes. Gladys used to play, hadn't she? Gladys Miles.

RF: What sort of music?

EA: Old songs. 'Take Me Home Kathleen,' and all things like that.

JA: "Peggy O'Neal".

RF: Did a lot of people go?

JA: Yes.

EA: They used to have musical nights in the Green Dragon. The Red Lion in Horsemarket was another one.

John Stevens (describing Scarletwell Street)

On one corner was a public house, 'The Crispin Arms'. On the opposite corner was a butcher's shop. On the diagonally opposite corner from the Crispin Arms was another pub, 'The Gate'. 'This gate hangs well and hinders none, refresh and pay and journey on.' That was the (motto).

With so many pubs it was not altogether surprising to hear tell of drunkenness and its consequences. Elsie Bull remembers, from her childhood in St. Mary's Street:

If you went round the corner of the street there was always drunks. Didn't matter what time of the day. We used to have to come by the public house as we come down King Street from home. Matter of fact, mother made us come the other way – round College Street and down St. Katherine's Street – because we didn't have to pass a pub. They were ever so fussy, my parents were. But I don't think we were hurt by it, if you know what I mean.

Frank Masters, (born – 1924. Lived in Semilong).

Frank Masters: Even in those days it was a slightly dangerous place to be, particularly the Mayorhold on a Saturday night.

It was a regular sight, the Mayorhold, on a Saturday night. There was the police there with handcarts and as the drunks came out the public houses, they were literally piled on the handcart and wheeled to the Police Station, which I should think was in Dychurch lane in those days. They slept the night in the cells until they were kicked out the next morning.

Chris Casey: So that was quite a lively area, a downmarket part of town?

FM: Oh yes. They were working class, good-hearted lot, they just lived a bit rough you know. They liked a drink...

Reg Tero

We used to have our problems on the old Mayorhold. A few fist fights used to go on when the pubs turned out. It used to be more family feuds in those days. They'd sort of knock hell out of each other Saturday night and they'd all be in the pub again Sunday dinnertime, buying each other a beer. You never got any knives and bottles and boots. It were just fists.

Alf Humphrey

Alf Humphrey: Every Saturday night there used to be a fight when they chucked out the pub, the 'Green Dragon', – us kids would come to see it. Oh, they'd fight like hell! Then next morning they'd be waiting outside – with black eyes – friendly as hell, and go in the pub again. It was nearly every Saturday night on the Mayorhold.

Chris Casey: Would there be a big group of men fighting?

AH: Mostly one'd have an argument in the pub. They all had a ring round a point in the middle, nobody'd interfere. Then all of a sudden perhaps the coppers would arrive, and they all had to disperse.

It was mostly the men who went out for a drink, not the women so much. You didn't see men and women go out like you do today, together like, for drinking.

George and Phyllis Rolfe

George Rolfe: On the Mayorhold itself there was the Green Dragon, Kings Head and the Jolly Smokers. Up Bearward Street, there was three pubs up there.

Phyllis Rolfe: There was the Ram at the top.

GR: Just on the Mayorhold itself, what me and the boys used to generally

Photo courtesy Northampton Museums & Art Gallery.

The Green Dragon, 54 Bearward Street and Mayorhold, 1895.

The Spotted Dog,
Grafton Street, 1970.

do, we used to go in one and have a few, then go in another and have a few, then go in the other and have a few. Circle out and round.

Louis Peters: Did you have a 'local'?

PR: The Kings Head was our local really, wasn't it?

GR: We used all of them. The Jolly Smokers, she was a nice landlady there.

PR: Margaret Sherwin.

GR: You'd wait for it to open as soon as you left off work at night. If you walked in there, perhaps a gal'd come to serve you and Margaret would shout: "Who's that?" Well we two say so, and – "Pull us two pints and send some sandwiches in." I don't drink at all now. It's funny, ain't it? I used to be out every day and now I don't touch it.

LP: Did they stick to the legal opening hours? They didn't allow you to drink after hours?

PR: Some of them did, in another room at the back.

GR: It's all according to how many years. When I was young it was all the time, but, these later years, they was strict. You was all right if you were going to sup over time if you went in their home quarters. Then they couldn't do anything about it, could they?

LP: (To Mrs Rolfe) Did you used to go up the pub as much?

PR: I always used to go up. He used to go early and I used to go later on. I used to work at the Green Dragon, behind the bar.

LP: So they were popular meeting places?

GR: At one time they used to be rough. Like when George Ingram had the Kings Head. Some of the kip house wallies at the time used to run out of money and he used to let them have so much. As long as (he) got it back when they got paid, it was all right. Anybody causing any rough stuff there, he was soon over the bar. Not round the bar.

PR: He used to jump over the bar!

GR: Over and out! He wouldn't stand no nonsense.

PR: The Green Dragon was the worst place for fights, wasn't it?

GR: These Irish blokes go in there in the afternoon, then at night, of course, they've had their bellyful. Then they start. Oh, we had a rough do. It was a rough do, and all. She (Mrs. Rolfe) was behind the bar with this other woman, Bet Williams. I'm down in the games room playing cards with one or two others. It was in the week. There wasn't many about. All of a sudden these Irish started. Somebody came down to tell me. I went up to see if she was all right and, as I opened the door there was only a blinking tray being flashed and it just missed her and this other gal.

PR: We got down quick. It went over the top of our heads, just skimmed it like that.

GR: There was a free for all then.

PR: There was stools, tables...ooh!

GR: You've never seen nothing like it.

PR: The landlady was out for the count. She drank herself stupid with Guinness.

GR: Oh, it was a proper do, that. I don't know who phoned the police or what. I started in the bar and finished in the back room. I had a lucky escape really, 'cause they was packed in there and this big, burly Irish bloke picked this stool up by the legs and struck it down at me. I just happened to ram him a bit and caught it across the shoulders. If I'd have had it across the back of the neck I wouldn't have been here today.

PR: Oh, it were murder. Blood everywhere.

LP: There seems to have been quite a large Irish community here.

GR: Well, that was since the war, when they was working on the M1 and that. But I'm going back in, like, the late '20's. They were mostly Irish navvies, you know, oldish. There wasn't many young people. Nowadays they come over young, don't they? Well, you get the odd one or two in every nationality, don't you?

Dennis and Peter Verrechia

Dennis Verrechia: On Saturday night the police used to go round in pairs. 'Specially up Horsemarket, that way. They was good people. But (the men) could fight like lions. They used to fight a lot them days.

Richard Foreman: Why did they used to fight?

DV: Perhaps they had a pint or two. Went up, out of the house. I'll tell you something else about them and all. Sunday dinnertime, come out of the

Fishing party outside the Sportsman's Arms, 1926.

A Jolly Smokers outing, 1950's.

pub, out of the Twenty-Fives, out gambling on Grafton Square. Throwing pennies up in the air.

RF: And betting on how they would fall.*

DV: Yes

RF: So the people would gather on the street to do that?

DV: Yes. They used to fight like hell. 'Course I was only a kid, go down Grafton Square to see them have a fight.

Angela Connor: What about crime? Was there a lot of crime in the area?

Peter Verrechia: Not a lot, no. Just get the odd one or two people...you know, you more or less got the regular people doing it. If anything was done the police would say, "Well, he's done it."

AC: You remember the policemen in the area?

PV: Yes, I remember old Chinky and one or two more... Chinky the Copper. You could always guarantee at ten minutes to ten he'd walk along Harding Street to knock off on his shift, ten o'clock shift...any patrolman.

Kit Lack and Elsie Allen also remember the police.

Kit Lack: They used to walk around a lot. Used to try doors, factory doors...

Elsie Allen : Our young days, when we went bunny running, you'd walk up Abington Street and stop in one doorway ('til) "Come on! Quick! Here's the police!" They used to have capes. (You) used to get a corner of the cape, or the gloves...

Reg Tero adds:

If I were standing in the street with a gang of boys and girls, 10, 11, 12, 13, 14 years of age, at nights... We always used to stand round the lamp-post because it was light and it was warm. And if a policeman walked round the bottom of the street you'd all run out the top. And you'd done nothing.

Abington Street and that was on a Saturday and Sunday night, even before and during the war, you were never allowed to stand in gangs or stand looking in shop windows. The policeman come up and move you

**This game was known as 'Pitch and Toss'.*

on. You could keep walking – you could walk up and down all night – and he wouldn't say nothing to you. You got in a shop doorway, he'd have you out and move you on.

Ron George (born 1917)

Richard Foreman: Can you say how the children would react when the police came round where they'd be playing?

Ron George: They wouldn't see the kids about, the police.

RF: They'd just disappear?

RG: One were on guard – watching for the police. When the police got there they'd disappear.

Born in Ambleside in the Lake District, George Harding came to Northampton to work as a police constable in 1932, at the age of 21. After 4 years, he joined the C.I.D., rising eventually to the rank of Detective Chief Inspector. He remained with the Northampton Police Force until his retirement. Here he recalls his days, 'on the beat' in the Boroughs.

The majority of people in the Boroughs were very pro-police. The dear old souls that kept the little shops, where the policemen used to go in (and) spend half the time in there drinking tea. I even got on a disciplinary charge: idling and wasting my time drinking tea. (But) we learned a lot by this. You go into the shop, through into the back room and the old person – usually elderly – would make some tea and we'd sit down. We would listen and they would talk. They knew everybody in the district. Who were going to have a baby, you know, the girls... The shop was a centre and a hub of everything. They all went to the shop. On Sundays they took their tray of potatoes, Yorkshire pudding and what-not down to the local bakery. They (the bakers) knew everybody. If somebody was spending a few bob that he shouldn't have, they would quite readily tell the police. They didn't consider themselves as grasses or informers, they just thought it was against the law, what they're doing, and you ought to know. By visiting these places we got no end of information.

Stephanie Record: What particular crimes were there? Was it just petty thieving?

GH: Mostly petty. A little bit of house breaking. In those days all those old houses had coin installed gas meters, electricity meters, where you put a shilling in. They were ripped open regularly, week after week. They was always a target. There wasn't a lot of money about in those days of the Boroughs in the '30's. The pawn shops were very busy. But – meters, petty thieving, theft of chickens, fowls, batteries from motor cars, theft from motor cars and all sorts of things. A lot of this property went to the local pawn shop which was on Regent Square. As a result of them pawning a lot of these various things – small items of jewellery, clothing and that – we were able to clear most of it up. We always knew that the pubs in those days were rough dives, but they were always pro-police when I came here. They hadn't always been pro-police, and they're not all pro-police now. Some are.

(Doors were left) open and unlocked. We very rarely had to break a door down to go in and make an arrest. You just opened the door and went in, even if it was three in the morning. If you wanted to go in unexpectedly, nine times out of ten, you could open the front door. And send a policeman round to the back door, which was the bolthole. If you wanted to run away – straight into the arms of a big policeman.

There was hardly ever a reason to break down a door. If there was, it was very soon broken down. With or without a warrant. That was something I wasn't careful enough about at first. I used to do things that perhaps I shouldn't and I've had many sleepless nights having done something I shouldn't. I used to console myself with the fact that (it was) in the interest of justice, the public and the detection of crime. If somebody said, "You shouldn't have done that, Governor," I'd have said, "No, You're dead right. But the end justified the means. We've got the bloke locked up."

Saturday nights, we always used to patrol the Boroughs in pairs. Two P.C.s 'til midnight. Well, (there were) pub fights, outside pubs, straight up fist fights. The Irishmen versus somebody. Even the women. Old Kate Robbins used to live down there and she'd come out the pub and take the town on when she'd had a few.

The practice was – it took me a little time to learn it, fresh from training school – you stood, back in a doorway, when they started to fight. You watched it for 5 minutes until it was nearly over and that was the best time to intervene. Then pack them off home, or take them. If you interfered at the beginning of a fight you'd get involved in it. I mean, you can't do it today, 'cause of the dangers. But then we many-a-times saw two drunks fighting outside a pub at closing time. Just hang on 'til they'd knocked the daylights out of each other. Then they were quite easy to handle.

The way the law was administered then was rather funny but could be very effectual. If, on occasions, we caught a couple in the back streets, misbehaving, shall we say... Fresh from training school, my training was, you arrested them and you charged them both with indecency or something like that. This old policeman said to me one day, he clouted this young man across the ear, gave the young girls a bit of good advice and off they went. I says, "Shouldn't we have arrested those two and taken them before the court?" He said, "Do you know what damage you do if you did that?" I said "No, tell me." He said, "The names go in the paper. They're both ashamed of themselves and the horrible publicity. You've ruined two homes, good parents, decent people who are also ashamed. And the neighbours begin to shun them. Look at the damage they've done, then they go to court and they fine them ten shillings each. You tell me, my boy, what have you achieved?" He said, "I've clouted them both and they've gone. If they're going to go and do something similar tomorrow night, they'll go. You'll not prevent it by taking them to court." And I often thought about that, a lot. They accepted a good hiding in those days, which they wouldn't today.

(Speaking of small-time Boroughs criminals) One thing about those sort of people – violence was abhorrent to them. They hated violence. In a bit of stealing, petty thieving, call it what you like, they'd run away rather than injure anybody. Now, the object appears to be, the slightest resistance – out comes the knife, or a club or whatever. That rather puzzles me. Those fellows, they were terrified. The policeman could clout them across the ears. They didn't resent that. They took it as a matter of course. If they got cheeky, we gave them one. And the next day they were quite happy about that, even after, if they'd been arrested. They respected it.

These characters, what we used to like about them as policemen: we gave many of them a shilling you see – that was either two pints of beer or three cups of tea and a cheese roll. We used to help them and they would have helped us. And did help us in anything serious. If there was a murder enquiry or something of a serious nature, attacks on little kiddies or girls, they would be the first to come along and give us some information.

Nobody dared make a complaint against the police in those days. I remember Freddy Allen, that slept out around the Boroughs. He went to court for petty theft, clothes or something and said, "I want to complain Your Honour, Your Worship, or whatever... Mr. Harding thumped me." And the Magistrate then – who's now long gone – said, "Take him out of the court. Coming here making insolent remarks like that." The truth was, of course, I had thumped him. And he was taken out, end of story, you see. But it would be rather different today, wouldn't it?

CHAPTER 6 – "PLENTY OF DIVERSIONS"
– Life in the Streets

Josephine Kent and Irene Swainsbury.

Julia Bush: Did you ever get musicians coming and playing in the streets?

Josephine Kent: Down on the Mayorhold, they used to come down there. On Sunday mornings there used to be a man come with a dancing bear and a violin. It wasn't every Sunday, some Sundays he used to come. He used to play this violin and the bear used to dance.

JB: Did you ever get any barrel organs come round?

JK: They used to come down the Mayorhold when I was a little girl. Again not very often. We used to walk behind them.

JB: Do you remember ice cream sellers?

JK: I can remember Walls' ice cream coming around with the old, blue bike. 'Stop me and buy one.' The other one was Seaby's. You used to get a penny ice lolly and it used to be in a triangle with blue and white check covering on the outside.

Irene Swainsbury: I know if we had a chocolate ice cream, we used to have one between us. They used to be tuppence, but that was a lot of money, so me and my brother used to have half each.

And I can remember – they used to come round sometimes and collect rags – and they used to give you a fish. A goldfish in a drop of water. That was like instead of giving you money for any rags that you'd got. It'd be in a little bag...

John Short

They used to come round with ice creams. Sometimes they'd have an ice cream barrow, you know, pushing it – two wheeled barrows. Or sometimes they'd have an ice cream cart with a pony on it. One of the first that came round was a family called Verrechia. They lived in Cooper Street. The same people: they only had ice cream in the summer. In the winter they'd have roast chestnuts on the Market Square. Used to do a good business there, but of course that's all gone.

Dennis Verrechia was born in 1895 at a house in Fetter Street. His parents came from Italy and started the family ice cream business in Northampton. His father would take home-made ice cream in a seven gallon freezer, on a pony and cart, all over the countryside – going sometimes as far as Buckingham. Dennis and his wife took over the business and, in his younger days, their son – Peter – helped out.

Dennis Verrechia: Years ago, they used to call ice cream Hokey Pokey you know. Weren't such a thing as wafer biscuits then. Used to be wrapped up in paper.

Angela Connor: How did people know that you were coming?

Peter Verrechia: He used to shout.

DV: 'All ices! – All ices!' like that I used to shout.

Richard Foreman: Did the business change much over the years?

DV: No. It never changed. I'm talking about when ice creams were a penny each. You had a wafer for a penny. I'm talking about before the First War.

RF: Did you have to put the prices up as time went on?

DV: Never went above tuppence. I used to get a living. It was poor, but we got one. Managed to bring six of them up on it. I've driven the pony home at 11 o'clock at night. 14 miles.

RF: Did you used to go round the Boroughs area?

DV: Oh yes. I always started off at the Boroughs and worked my way along through the Mayorhold up to Kingsthorpe. I always come up to Kingsthorpe, on Sundays and I always reckoned that was the best part of Northampton for taking money at anything. Public houses. Everything. It always seemed the best part of the town to take money.

RF: How was the ice cream kept cold?

DV: It was ice, packed round it. It was iced cream them days.

RF: Did your family make it?

DV: Yes.

RF: How was it made?

DV: In a big container… with milk, eggs, not like today. It was made with milk them days. That's what you used to call ice cream, not like today. You can't get nothing like that today.

PV: Made with eggs wasn't it dad?

DV: Yes, them eggs my mother used, they were Egyptian eggs. They used to come in a big flat basket. 18 to a shilling them days. Only little eggs they were.

RF: Did you sell anything else apart from ice cream?

PV: Well, we used to stand with the hot potatoes (in the winter). Mother used to have the flowers. My wife... I'm talking about some years ago – we used to have paregoric cough tablets. They'd be about 30 a packet. Had a duty on it and that finished it. Couldn't sell 'em. We looked at anything at the time and tried to get rid of it.

Bill Coulson

Milk deliveries. That was done by a chap with a pony and trap. (He had) his large milk churns on the trap and transferred it to a small hand can that he brought to the door and measured out the milk into jugs. On Sundays, during wintertime, a man would call round selling shellfish. (He'd) just open the door and let you know he was there by shouting. In the afternoon another chap came round selling watercress. He opened the door (and) bellowed up the passage, "Watercreesy." (Laughs) – to which was replied either, "Half a mo, I'm coming." or "Bugger off." That was the jingle cry.

Jim and Pat Edwards

Jim Edwards: There was the knife sharpener used to have a barrow sort of thing and some had a bike. He put the bike on a stand and he'd got the grindstone in front where his handlebars was. He could put a belt from the back wheel – which was off the ground, on a stand – to the grindstone. He used to come round, "Any knives or shears to sharpen?"

The rag and bone man used to come round. They was the regular ones. They use to come round and shout, "Rags, bones, bottles." He used to use the bones. Boil them up I suppose.

Pat Edwards: I can remember the man that sold winkles, with a wooden barrow going round Compton Street. People used to have winkles for their tea on Sunday.

JE: Used to get half a pint of winkles. Like a half pint measure they have in a pub. Used to dip (it) in the bucket or basket and put them in your bowl. You'd all sit round the table on a Sunday afternoon with your pin and get the winkles out. One of my sisters used to have a winkle sandwich. Two bits of bread and butter and put all the winkles on them (laughs). They had others, mussels, whelks, but we always used to go for winkles.

John Stevens.

I can remember a man coming round with a performing bear. 'See the bear catch the pole' and he used to throw this pole that the bear catches. I can remember barrel organs coming round. Saturday afternoons was the playtime for people. I can remember groups of Dr. Barnardo's boys coming and singing in the streets, to advertise the home and hopefully collect money.

Richard Foreman: It's been mentioned that there was sometimes a blind violinist who used to play around Christmas time.

JS: Blind Teddy. I can't tell you much about him but I can remember him. There used to be a blind man also who brought a barrel organ around.

RF: Blind Bellamy was it?

JS: Yes. There used to be the occasional bands of Scottish Pipers come down and dance the sword dance in the street. Almost every other Saturday afternoon there used to be what they used in those days to call an Archery Tournament. They used to sell prize draw tickets. You bought a book of tickets for about a shilling and you got 13 or 14 and if you paid a penny you got one. And there were perhaps a dozen prizes. All of this as a means of supporting someone who'd had something unfortunate happen. There used to be a lot of consumption about in those days, you see, and people had to be supported and there was no other way of getting money for them. That gave people lots of diversion.

RF: Were there any particular streets where these things would happen?

JS: So far as I know they used to make up their minds which were the places, you know, like the old tramps: and in those days tramps used to come through the streets. And of course, cattle were driven through the streets see, there was no transportation of cattle, or very little tranportation of cattle on the railway, they were all walked on the hoof from their fattening grounds down to the various slaughter places.

KW: Didn't they used to drive them down Bell Barn Street?

JS: That's true, yes. This butcher that I mentioned, Bullocks – every Wednesday they used to have a slaughter day, and we used to go straight from school, straight down there, and pull on the rope, pull the bullock's head down. Ha, ha. Diversions, you know.

Broad Street – with Regent Street and the Albion pub on the right.

Residents of Grafton Place gather on waste ground to celebrate the 1935 Jubilee.

Joyce Hall

They'd drive the cattle up Horsemarket from the cattle market, into this butcher's shop and they were all slaughtered at the back. One day, when they were driving them up, one of the cows broke away and ran up King

Street and down our yard. Petrified. So we all ran into the house. It was mad or something. My father shut the shop door and there was this cow bellowing in our yard. They had to fetch someone from the cattle market to come and get hold of it, put a rope around its neck and drag it away. Another time, one of them escaped in St. Katherine's churchyard and that was really mad. It chased round and round the church in circles. We saw this cow with its head down, bellowing and going mad. They had to shoot it. Down my father's yard and shop, there was a little window at the back of his workshop that looked into the churchyard. I remember, as children, we all stood up and looked through this little window at this man who had to stand on the wall and shoot this cow.

Ken and Mary Smith

Ken Smith: My father came up and put the lines down for the trams and he was here when he helped take them up.

Mary Smith: Hadn't they – if I remember right – wooden seats? Slatted seats.

KS: Sit up the top. Teeming with rain – used to sit up top... They was all right in them days 'cause things were slower. You've got buses today 'cause things are quicker. They were devils 'though, on a pushbike if you got in one of them lines. It's a hell of a job getting out of them. All Saints were the worst. Round All Saints there were lines going all ways, you had to be ever so careful. It'd fetch you off. I was an errand boy, you see, used to have to go up there a lot. Used to have to be ever so careful.

Kate Wills: And they wouldn't stop for you?

KS: No. They just used to keep ringing the bell all the while. Ding, ding. ding.

John Short

The dustcarts: they used to come round with a tip-cart. A two-wheeler that used to tip up, to unload the load, and tip back. But the Borough dustcarts they were a bit bigger than the farmers' carts and they used to take all the town rubbish to Castle Street to the Destructor, you see. And there was no dustbins. I don't know whether dustbins had been invented then. You used to have a wooden box, or cardboard boxes...anything. We used to call them ashboxes, not dustboxes because everybody had ashes from the fires in those days.

Coal carts. There was a continual stream of coal carts coming out of the railway depot at St. Andrews Road. I should think there was about 20 coal merchants in the town in those days and some of them would have quite a number of carts and horses. Four wheelers. Only one horse. And they'd pull about a ton of coal.

The horse drays used to have a chain horse to get up Black Lion Hill from the goods yard. Because it was cobbles you see, and they couldn't get a footing on the cobbles. They used to slip and down they used to go sometimes.

Grose's buses. At the end of the war Grose's started a bus service. Double deckers. And they ran to Market Harborough, Weedon, Daventry and Stony Stratford. They were blue buses. That was before the United Counties came along. I wouldn't say they were the first because there were some people name Beedon on the corner of London Road... There were various local buses.

Grose's terminus was in the top end of St. Andrews Road. There's a big wall. That's where they used to stop. That's where I learned to cycle down that hill in St. Andrews Road, when I was 12. My friend's brother was in the army. He came home one leave and he bought Tom a little boy's bike. We was only 11 or 12 see? And that's where I learned to ride going down St. Andrews Road. I got on this bike and I went down the hill on my own. There were no motors about.

I was 17 before I got my own bike. I bought it after I started work. Lovely bike. Cost me 17 guineas. B.S.A.

There was people used to come round the streets with a timber wagon. This was in the spring. And they'd have a load of bean sticks, pea sticks and line props. They (line props) was about a shilling. They came from the country. Silverstone or Hartwell or somewhere like that. Where the woods were.

CHAPTER 7 – 'THAT WAS YOUR EVENING'S ENTERTAINMENT'

Pat Edwards

Summer evenings people used to sit on the step and that was your evening's entertainment. You'd take your knitting or sewing and sit on the step or a chair. They'd sit on their own doorsteps. But they'd all shout across and all go and sit near each other. (It would) be just like a little family session.

Edna Brown

EB: (asked about memories of major events in her childhood). The only thing I can remember is when the crystal radio set first came. We had nothing until Dad bought one of those. But only one person could sort of hear it, at that particular time. You had earphones. It was very tricky to get going.

Jim Edwards

JE: There was the little garage where we used to take the accumulators for charging up. For your radio. You had a wet battery, similar to a car battery. About four inches square by six inches deep with a little carrying handle. And the red and black connectors on the top where you used to connect (it) to your radio. They was about tuppence to charge them up I think. Took about 24 hours. We used to have two. Put one on and have one on charge.

Ron Draper

RD: Oh yes. I can remember when Wireless Relay came. They used to advertise 'Wireless Without Worry'. That was their slogan, and it was true.

Ron Johnson: What did they do?

RD: Well, all you had was a speaker. They must have picked up the signal from somewhere and relayed it from Horsemarket. The signal was fantastic – I mean you couldn't get nothing like it on a battery set. If you had an electric set, all you got was everybody's bloody sewing machine. But you didn't get a lot on relay. Lovely that was – one and sixpence a week. 'Course then they turned over to Rediffusion – a different company

altogether.

Lucy Starmer

In 1926, the General Strike, people who'd got these wirelesses got the news. Well, us who'd only got Cat's Whisker, we didn't get the news. That was awful to my father. So, after the General Strike was over, we persuaded him to buy a wireless. He went to someone down Horsemarket, a garage it was, Caves. I think we had the highest wireless mast in our garden. If Pa did anything, he did it to perfection.

They fixed it for him on a Saturday afternoon. Pa always worked for the Friendly Society on a Saturday afternoon, much to the displeasure of his staff. But, you see, he was a divisional secretary and he'd got all these village secretaries under him and they come into town to see him on a Saturday.

So, he come home for tea, Saturday afternoon, and when he come in the room he said, "We're not going to keep that!" 'Cause it was a big loudspeaker and a box arrangement (about two feet by two feet). They'd put it in the windowsill. 'Cause at our old Post Office they were wide windowsills. You could sit in the windows. So he said, "That can go back. Hiding the light like that!" Anyway the next morning I switched it on for him and it was a church service. It was a special one from the Foundling Hospital in London. Of course, as soon as it started, Pa said, "Twenty years since I've heard a church service."

And then they ended up with the Hallelujah Chorus. I'll never forget it. The tears were coming down his cheeks, because he was brought up on the Messiah in his family Sunday evenings. And it was never going back, never going back...

But we fixed it. We picked a bit out of the wall (for the) side of the wireless. And he had every improvement. Anything came in, he had it improved. He'd always got it on. And after he retired, it was all day long. The talks and everything. Not just the music then.

Josephine Kent

JK: Used to have to play your half hour's music. Used to go to Miss Palmer's, up Military Road. Sixpence a lesson it used to be, twice a week. Tuesdays and Saturday. It was a lot of money in those days.

Julia Bush: Your parents were very keen on music were they?

JK: My father was a singer. He sang under the name of Jim Carne. He was very well known in the town.

JB: Where did he sing?

JK: He used to go out on all the clubs, go out to Leicester and all the way round. He'd got a beautiful voice.

Irene Swainsbury: He had a top hat didn't he?

JK: Oh yes. Evening wear. If he went out of town to sing, I can remember my sister going down the station with his working clothes on a Monday morning and he'd change in the station and then go on to work. She'd bring his evening clothes home.

JB: Can you remember what he used to sing?

JK: He used to sing all the ballads. 'Because', that used to be one, 'Take You Home Again, Kathleen' and 'Marta'... He'd got a marvellous voice.

George and Phyllis Rolfe

Louis Peters: Where did you go dancing?

George Rolfe: Well, down the Salon, I think it was then.

Phyllis Rolfe: And one down Kingsthorpe Hollow, the Tivoli.

GR: One the bottom of College Street. The Premier. That was a rough one.

PR: Me and my friend, we used to go to Weedon, to the Globe Hotel. All the soldiers used to go down there.

GR: But that one, the bottom of College Street, you couldn't dance to save your life because there was too many in there. Packed like sardines. I went twice. First time I went, I cleared the floor. I was dancing with this Land Army girl. A bloke sees me, up this dancehall, this Saturday night. I had a bit of a barny with (him) when I was working at the Corporation (and) he took a nark. As I was dancing round, I saw this fist coming at me. So I pushed this Land gal, as much as I could, into the crowd, out the road, and I ducked. Of course, I let fly didn't I, quick, naturally. Before you could say 'Jack Robinson' the floor was cleared and the police had got us. 'Course, just inside the door, – there was two doors, two entrances – used to be a couple of coppers, at each one. They took us outside and wanted to know what was what. So he said to this bloke, "Look, get off, before I take you on." He said to me, "You can go back inside. I watched you. I seen him sling you a punch."

PR: When he was younger, he didn't ask questions. He hit first, and then asked.

GR: That's how you're brought up. You'd got to get first in every time.

LP: Was dancing a regular thing? Did you go every week?

PR: Well, there was dances every night really, at different places. The Salon – it's Cinderella or something now – then, the corner of College Street, above the billiard hall. There used to be dancing in Fish Street. You could go to a dance every night of the week, different places. used to be another big one up against Abington Park.

Mary Smith

Mary Smith: I remember the roller skating rink in Broad Street.

Ken Smith: When did that start up?

MS: Sometime in the early '30's, perhaps about '33 or '4. I used to sit up in my bedroom window and I could look out and watch them. Mostly (on) Saturdays, they used to have dances on the roller skates, fancy dress parties and things.

KW: Did anyone ever come to grief?

MS: Oh yes, I should think nearly every time it was on they'd have the ambulance there. Someone would go off with a broken leg or a broken arm. But the thing was, it was just at the bottom of our garden. When they had these fancy dress things, the things we found the next day... Swords and all sorts of things.

Reg Tero

You could go to the cinema at night for thruppence, tuppence even. I mean, the old St. James Cinema over near the Dover Hall, Saturday afternoons that was a penny. They didn't even bother to let you go in the office door, you know; the main foyer. They used to open one of the fire exits at the side and a fellow used to stand there with a stocking in his hand and you used to drop your penny in and go in.

We had a lot of cinemas in them days. The St. James Cinema finished up as the Roxy and then we had the Temperance Hall up Newland. We had the Exchange; the place is still there where they do the bingo. We had the Cinema De Luxe in Campbell Street, the Majestic at the corner of Gold Street. It was built on the front, but the actual shell of the cinema is still down there, it was never taken away.

We'd got quite a few cinemas and we'd vary you know. 'Cause it wasn't too far to walk to any of them. Whoever had got the best cowboy film on, you went. If it had got something else, you didn't bother, but if it was cowboys and indians you went. Buck Jones and a few more.

John Stevens

John Stevens: Used to be a cinema at the bottom of Gold Street where Bells showroom is now. Used to be another one in Gold Street between the bottom of College Street and Boots corner, used to be a cinema there, called the Pavilion, there was one just over the Westbridge at a corner of a street. Whittons the last makers have a place on the corner there now. Dovers used to have a place there and there was a skating rink. It used to be a skating rink and I think, whether that passion died out quite quickly or was too expensive for people to keep up, they turned it into a cinema. There were various others came later on in the scene but they were the chief ones in the town.

Richard Foreman: Which ones would the Boroughs children go to most?

JS: From our area they would go to the Temperance Hall, which is in Newland, where the Grosvenor is now.

RF: Can you remember what it was like inside?

JS: Oh yes. It was flat inside with some seats and some standing up room.

Used to play the piano and pretend they were galloping horses and all this sort of thing. And you used to watch your opportunity to crawl underneath to get a seat. I think you paid tuppence if you had a seat and you paid a penny to stand. Used to see 'The Exploits of Elaine', and 'The Clutching Hand', and all that sort of thing.

Kit Lack and Elsie Allen

Kit Lack: We used to go to the Cinema De Luxe, up Campbell Street. They were silent films when we went, 'cause – when our gran used to go with my cousin – she used to have to read out to her what it had got on it.

Richard Foreman: So the whole family went along.

Elsie Allen: The oldest cinema in this town was the Temperance Hall. We knew the man who part kept it – him and his brother – and we used to have some free tickets, Saturday night, for the circle.

We went to the Majestic, to see 'Mr Woo'. There were no seats when we got there, so they let us in with no seats. We had an upturned ladder. Row of kids sitting on it. You know what it's like – kept going down, kept coming up...

And it was exciting really, because he has to commit hari kiri. I didn't understand any of it – I weren't sharp enough. But I always remember this 'Mr Woo'.

At the finish of it (the ladder) went flop, so of course none of us kids along there would come out. We were getting on – might have been 14, I don't know. We went and sat down. He came to see our tickets and we said we hadn't seen the picture properly. So they let us stop and see it a second time.

John Short

The only picture I remember seeing was Pearl White in 'The Clutching Hand'. A hand used to come on... No orchestra. Only a piano; and he used to play that piano like mad.

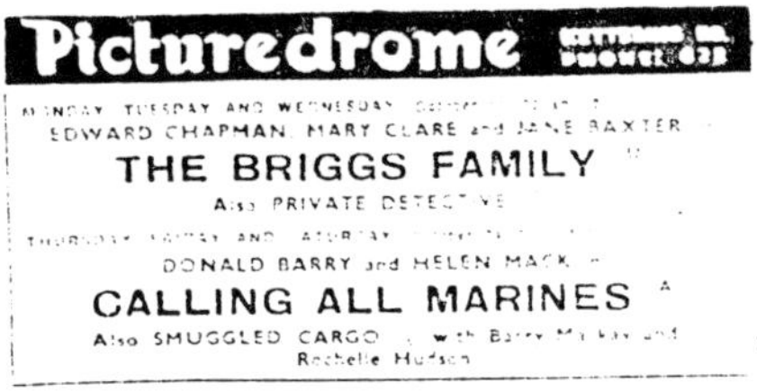

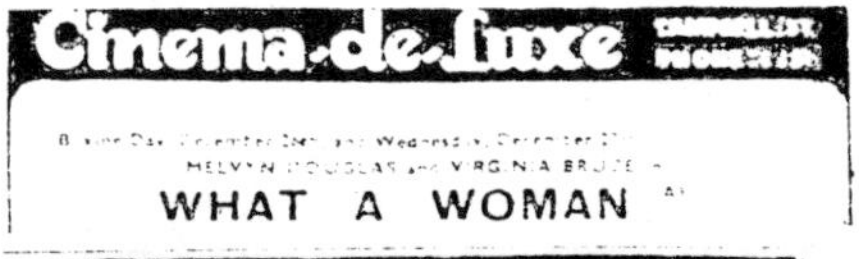

CHAPTER 8 – 'APTLY CALLED CHARACTERS'

Bob Stanton: There were several people, or more aptly called characters, whose names were a household word, and if people can still talk about them after 60 years or so, they must have had something.

Blind Bellamy

Elizabeth Whitney: There used to be a blind man in Grafton Street. There used to be some little streets led off there: Todds Lane, Gilbert Lane... Used to be a blind man there with a barrel organ and he used to go round playing. And his grand-daughter... She used to go round with him, 'cause he were blind.

John Short: He used to come round. He employed a man to pull the organ and he helped pull it with a bit of rope tied on the side. My mother used to give him a cup of tea. But he was about the town for a long time. He was well known about the town. There was another barrel organ that used to be round the town and that was pulled by another man named Someo. He was an Italian that came in the town and afterwards, this Someo family they got good jobs in trade and industry and were quite well off really.

(The barrel organists) had regular routes. They'd stop outside a certain house and play. The man – not the blind man, but the man who pulled the organ – would go round with a tin of some sort. Used to rattle it up and down. I suppose he'd get out and he'd earn a penny there and that was it. I don't think there was any blind institute in those days. He was one of the well-known characters in the town, of which there were several.

Newton Pratt

Reg Tero: Used to be a fellow called Newt Pratt in the town. He's dead and gone now. He was a horse dealer. There was a public house down Scarletwell Street called the Friendly Arms, owned by a Mr. Sewell, in those days, Bill Sewell. And this fellow, Newt Pratt, used to bring a zebra down there on a Sunday dinner time. Used to tie it up outside and he used to give it beer. Bring a jug of beer out to it.

'Tommy Mangle-the-Cat'

Ron George: There was a chap the bottom of Bath Street, we used to call him 'Tommy Mangle-the-Cat'. If you went after him, he used to chase (you).

Richard Foreman: He would chase the kids?

RG: They were calling him that name – 'Tommy Mangle-the-Cat'. Whether he put a cat through the mangle I don't know. That was the slogan.

Mr. Perrin – The Lamplighter

Bob Stanton: Next to Teddy's Row was Perrin's sweet shop. Mr. Perrin was the lamplighter and when he came out with his long pole, that was the signal to go out and close the shutters and then start getting ready for bed. A lot of houses had shutters which were like two small doors that closed across the front windows. They made the room very cosy in the winter – as good as double glazing.

Len Riley: We used to play him up! There was only one lamp in Herbert Street and one at the top – and as soon as he'd lit a lamp we'd shin up the lamp-post and blow it out (laughs).

Kate Wills: What sort of apparatus did he use?

LR: He used to have a long pole, about six foot/seven foot long. I don't know what he kept for a light but it was shielded so that it didn't go out. He used to push up the glass trap door like, and turn the gas on with a hook and light the gas.

KW: Did he live locally?

LR: He lived on the Mayorhold, in the sweet shop. He used to spend his daytimes going round these lamp-posts, climbing up and cleaning them, washing them all down. It was a full time job for him. He used to have to go out every day to do them and light them in the evening as soon as it got dark and go round in the morning and put them out.

Jim Allard: We used to follow him about. And I said, "Hooray!" every time he lit the lamp.

Black Charley

John Short: He lived in one of the courts in Scarletwell Street and he was jet black and absolutely white his hair. And I should imagine in those days he must have been about 60. But he was bent and he went round with a trolley which was all tied up with ropes and the wheels – instead of tyres, they'd got ropes tied on. And he used to get his living out of dustbins, getting rags and bones. His wife was a little white woman and they had a fair sized family and they were all coloured. But I seem to remember the oldest one was white. The oldest girl. There's still some of the family about.

Ron George was the son of Black Charley. He was born in 1917. His father died in 1926, and Ron had in his possession a paper which gave the following information:

> There was buried from the Northampton Poor Law Institution on April 28th, 1926 an aged full-blooded negro named Henry George who died from pleurisy.
>
> He had been an inhabitant of Northampton for over thirty years and was a well-known figure as he went about his occupation ... in a very humble way. He answered to the general sobriquet of 'Black Charley' and was of a quiet, inoffensive disposition. He was admitted to the local Poor Law Institution about a month ago.
>
> Uneducated and of meagre mental capacity, his age was more or less a matter of conjecture. Officially he was 78 but this possibly was an under-estimate by several years.
>
> Born in slavery of slave parents on an American plantation 'way down Tennessee,' he was one of the many who were freed by United States Congress in 1863. He bore on his left shoulder his brand of slavery, which was presumably the brand of the owner of the plantation on which he was born, and where he afterwards worked. This brand was a scroll surmounted by two triangles separated by double lines, of which the subjoined is a rough sketch.

Richard Foreman: Your father used to collect rags and bones. Where did he sell them?

Ron George: There used to be a rag and bone merchant on Bull Head Lane. That used to be Rathbones.

He used to go out. Wandering. Walked all back and forwards... all over the place. Kislingbury, Duston... all round. (Sometimes he) wouldn't come back (for a) long while. My mother told me he used to go to lodging houses. One lodging house he went in, this chap used to tip him upside down on the fire. Punched him in the eye. Come at him with a frying pan.

Evelyn Gammage: You'd be the only black family up there (the Boroughs). Did they still include you, help you and make you feel welcome?

RG: Yes. Never had any enemies.

My father was a staunch Christian, a firm believer. Used to see him in a barn. People used to see him on his hands and knees, praying, in barns and that. Anywhere.

Richard Foreman: When your father arrived in Britain, was Northampton the first place he lived?

RG: I imagine he'd been up in Wales. (My mother) came from Abergavenny.

RF: Did your father have any close friends, people he saw a lot of?

RG: When he got out on the road and that, you don't know who he might see. They could all be friends couldn't they? But he was a lonesome bird.

The family lived in Forecourt, off Scarletwell Street. Later, after 1926, they moved to Bath Street. Ron's mother, Selina, whom he described as a short woman, with extremely long hair, was many years younger than her husband and died at the age of 76 in 1954.

Elsie Allen: I used to see Black Charlie and I used to go terrified, running alone. I were frightened to death of dark people. Scared stiff of them. Then, when I was 14, I went to see 'Uncle Tom's Cabin'. I thought they were wonderful.

Kit Lack: Oh yes, Black Charley was the first one. We used to say to our Dad, "Who're you going to vote for, Dad?" And he used to say, "Black Charley, Lord Mayor of Scarletwell Street."

Mary Jane

Jim Allard: Poor old Mary Jane. She were a woman what finished up round here.

Eileen Allard: Didn't she used to do a bit of this? (Imitates a fighter.) Like a man. She could fight like the next man.

Phyllis Rolfe: Mary Jane used to always strip off to her camisole... She's dead now, but I've seen her fight.

George Rolfe: Any man there was. Not just women. Any man there was – there she is on the Mayorhold.

PR: And if she hadn't finished it Saturday night, she'd be up there Sunday morning to finish it.

A Well Known Landlord

Josephine Kent: He lived in the Boroughs. He used to have a lot of houses to rent and, if people didn't pay, he had them out.

Irene Swainsbury: He always rode a bike.

JK: That's right, a big bike.

Julia Bush: How did he get people out?

JK: Well, there was no choice then. If you didn't pay your rent you had to move out. You weren't covered by the law, them days, His property always used to be a little run down, hadn't it?

IS: Very run down.

Elizabeth Whitney: ...He was a well-known landlord. He used to ride about on an old lady's bike. Didn't look as if he had two ha'pennies for a penny. He owned no end of property in Northampton, round this way...

Jim Edwards: Always used to wear a dirty old coat.

EW: Coat and hat and old lady's bike. And he wouldn't do no repairs.

Mrs. Evans

Greta Matthews: Mrs. Evans lived in Bell Barn. She had a yard, with a cow which Mr. Evans took out to graze in the day. It came back in the evening, was milked and then the milk was sold. People took jugs. We used to joke and say Mr. Evans milked the cow under a tree when it rained, so we got half milk and half rain water. Also in the yard were ducks, with water in a tin bath.

Saved Every Sunday!

Elizabeth Whitney: We used to go to the Salvation Army, that was down Guildhall Road, and along Angel Lane, there used to be the Young People's Citadel. We used to go up some steps. We used to go up there Sunday nights. We was about 12 or 13. We used to sit and sing. Then they'd say, 'Will you come to the front and be saved?' Well, there used to be one woman – used to sell papers on Mercer's Row – and every Sunday she'd go to the front to be saved. And she'd cry. And we'd start laughing.

Like Mrs. Noah

Joan G. Maggs: (Writing in response to the Living Memory Project's exhibition at Abington Park Musem, September 1986)... it turned my thoughts back to my own childhood and a 'charlady/washerwoman' my mother employed, who came from Scarletwell Street. We lived in the old Barracks (1920-35).

This lady was small and rotund (like Mrs. Noah) and had numerous children. Also a husband who drank rather more than his share of Phipps' Ale.

She used to take our sheets home to wash and sometimes they didn't come back as promised. When my eldest brother was sent round to Scarletwell Street he found they'd been pawned and Mrs P-- hadn't got the cash to redeem them! Poor soul. I don't know how it was resolved. Possibly my mother advanced her the money out of her next week's wage.

Mr. Roberts

John Stevens: Nellie Worrall, she was the grand-daughter of a man named Roberts and he was the last clay pipe maker in the country, I believe. And he lived, and his workshop was in Scarletwell Street. In Scarletwell Street there were two jitties, one of them was called Pipe Maker's Yard, the pipe makers were at the corner you see. Mr. Roberts had that place. Only women worked for him. They used to make the clay pipes and he used to take them round the public houses in all of Northamptonshire in the car.

Elizabeth Whitney: There used to be an old man in Scarletwell Street and he used to make clay pipes. Well, I couldn't have been very old then. I can remember that I used to go and buy these clay pipes for bubbles, about a farthing each (broken).

Nurse Fryer

Bob Stanton: Nurse Fryer, a rather forbidding figure with her flowing cape or coat, long black skirt, bonnet on her head, and leather Gladstone bag, all perched on a sit-up-and-beg type ladies bicycle.

Rev. Fielding Daniels

Bob Stanton: A tall man who put the fear of God and the devil combined into anyone who crossed his path, with his hat flat on his head, longish coat, leggings and large boots. He was against drinking in public houses and drinking generally and at every opportunity made it known. But his red face and large bluish nose gave the impression of being the reverse in private. It was said at the time it was his persistance that closed the Sewing Machine public house, at the bottom of Regent Street. As, in his opinion, there were more in there at times than in his church. (St. Andrews).

One Sunday lunchtime he turned the corner into St. Andrews Street by the Grafton Arms. There was a young lad standing outside. This, he must have thought, was an easy victory, but not so. "Where's your father?" he said to the lad. "In the pub." he replied. "And where's your mother?" he asked. "In the pub." he replied. "And where's your dinner then?" The answer came straight back, "Across the road in Tee's bakehouse."

Mr. Malone

Bob Stanton: Malone, the official rat catcher, used to walk across the Mayorhold wearing a flat cap, brown smock with his box of ferrets slung over his shoulder and his three small terriers trotting at the side of him. He had a tame white rat which he had in his coat pocket when he went out for a drink.

Photo courtesy Mr. Terry Malone.

Mr Malone, 1926.

Kate Wills: And what about the Ratcatcher, who emptied a sack of 30 rats and set the dog on them?

Len Riley: I can't recall his name, lived in Regent Street. His mate came up with the (sack) and I think they had a bet on how many (the dog) could kill. And he took this sack and emptied it. (The rats) spread out but they hadn't gone many yards before that dog got them. Got the lot bar one and that run down towards Drum Lane and that's where he caught it up. He just kicked it up the backside (laughs). It killed it, I saw that myself.

Peter Verrechia: You tell them about Mick Malone, the rat catcher.

Dennis Verrechia: He'd kill a rat with his teeth. There used to be a public house in Horseshoe Street called the Harbour Lights. Sunday dinnertime they'd let one or two rats go in the bar. He'd kill them with his teeth. Just for a pint of beer. I've never seen it done but I've heard.

Freddy Allen

George Harding: Another little, famous character – Freddy Allen. He lived in the Boroughs. At least, he didn't live there, he slept there. These pictures we see, of fellows wrapped up in newspapers under the bridges and arches of London. Freddy used to sleep like that. Until a policeman came along and kicked him out and then he'd go around the corner and sleep somewhere else. He was another likeable villain, petty thief. Would pinch milk off the doorsteps, pinch the loaves of bread off the bread van and that's how he existed and lived for many years.

Nobby Clark

Bob Stanton: Nobby Clark used to live in Johnsons Row. He entered the hospital Cycle Parade every year and was well known as lots of people used to look for him in the Parade. He went in as Dirty Dick on one occasion, covered in dirt and dust with dirty, worn out clothing, pushing a barrow with his dog in it. His slogan was 'Ten years ago I used your soap, since then I've used no other,' with adverts for Pears soap on the barrow.

CHAPTER 9 – THIS AND THAT

The Destructor

John Stevens: When you get to Bath Street there was built, in the years almost prior to the 1914-1918 War, a square playing ground and that was built by the unemployed. That was one way of ameliorating their condition. Then a bit further down the street, there was the entrance to what we used to call the Destructor. All the rubbish from the town was taken here and burned and with that burning they produced steam which made the electricity to run the tram system... There was two entrances to that, one in Bath Street and one in Castle Street... then ultimately the Council sold that out to Northamptonshire Electricity.

Len Riley: You'd got just the towers or chimney which emitted all the smoke which usually blew down Horsemarket. Carts used to gather up all the boxes of rubbish and the driver was standing on the top. And then took (it) down to the incinerator, upended the cart and tipped it over like a chute. I've been in there and seen them when I was a kid. And you could see all the firing down below.

Transport

Bob Stanton: Mostly horse drawn, such as the L.M.S. drays and the coke carts which used to come up Horsemarket, across the Mayorhold and up Broad Street. If sufficient coke had not fallen off the cart, to be put on the fire, some lad would dive out from a hiding place and put a small block of wood under the rear wheel just to jolt the cart enough to shake some coke off.

Each year at August time, Bonhams used to loan some of their horses to the Territorials to pull the gun carriages down to the Castle Station to go on their annual camp.

J.B. Collier's Car

Irene Swainsbury: Mr. Collier lived in Sheep Street. One of the highlights of our week – I think it was on a Friday – was (when) he come home in a car. You know what cars were, them days! If any of us were in the street he'd stop at the top and give us a little ride down Bull Head Lane, up Bearward Street and back down. Then one of us would get out and open the garage door for him and he'd drive us in the garage. That was a highlight, when he came home and gave us a little ride in his car.

'Georgie Bumble's Office'

Richard Foreman: I was told there was a public toilet that was always known as 'Georgie Bumble's Office'.

Jim Allard: That were a grey place. I was seeing if I could buy it for scrap iron, but it was bloody made of slate.

RF: Who was Georgie Bumble? Did he work for the Borough?

JA: No. Old Georgie never worked for nobody. He were a moocher. Poor old Georgie Bumble. He come out of Spring Lane.

Lodging Houses

Richard Foreman: What sort of people used to live in the lodging houses?

Eileen Allard: Navvies most of them. They all used to meet in the Green Dragon.

Jim Allard: They stayed in the lodging house. The lodging house were about a shilling a night. A man named Jackson kept (it), cleaner than a pin. Good man. He'd change the beds all the while. That's as much as I know of the good old town.

George Rolfe: On the Mayorhold, and round there, was these kip houses. Mostly Irish blokes. They was rough and ready, with their old corduroy trousers and that. They used to get a kip for about sixpence a night. If they couldn't get a bed they could sleep on the floor cheaper. There was Althorp Street, top of Bath Street, Castle Street and I think there was one up Fore Street. Four, all in that little area, you see. Well, they used to be boozing. Work all day, booze all night – and then they used to start. Fights galore and everything.

The Blackshirts

George Rolfe: Just before the war, the Blackshirts had headquarters on the Mayorhold. They used to be a bit of trouble now and again. Moseley... One fellow, used to work on the railway, he was one of their chiefs. He lived about three doors away from me. But when the war broke out he had to go in the army, like.

Health

John Stevens: Children played in the streets you know. I think this is what immunised people like me against disease. You got into a lot of horse traffic in the street and it used to leave a certain residue. You played marbles in the gutter and skimming cigarette cards and that sort of thing. Of course you picked up everything. And so you got a little bit of everything into you so you never succumbed to anything.

Funerals

Josephine Kent: I can remember Bonhams the funeral people. I can remember the black horses with the plumes for the funerals, used to fascinate me. With the carriages.

Julia Bush: Did people have big funerals in the Boroughs?

JK: Oh yes. You was always buried properly.

Irene Swainsbury: (There) always used to be one person to lay the people out.

JK: When my Father died it was Mrs. Gibbs, lived down Scarletwell Street. She came to my Father. They used to go round, you see, and that was their job. It was to earn money. I don't know how much they used to be paid. But I can remember my Mother saying to me, "Go on, run and fetch Mrs. Gibbs." And I went down to the bottom of Scarletwell Street. Always put a clean pina on, she did. Spotlessly clean.

IS: But, I mean, there was no other funeral directors. Everybody had Bonhams.

JK: He was a friend of my Father's, Harry Bonham was. His mother, Ann Bonham, started the business up. She was in Broad Street. She lived on the opposite side and the horses were kept up the stables at the back. The shop itself was on the Mayorhold, where he used to do his business. I can remember the coffins used to be upstairs.

Lucy Starmer: When anybody died, the undertaker came. 'Course you never took them to the undertakers, they remained in the house. Well, my parents did. I wouldn't have dreamt of them going to an undertaker. And women did the job – they used to come and lay the corpse out. And the undertaker used to have these black boards, the length of the window right from the top to the (bottom). They'd put them on the windowsill. If the corpse was in the house they put the board near the door. But if it was a relative – you know: not in the house – they put it further away from the door. (They stayed) until the funeral was over.

The Fever Cart

John Short: Just along St. Andrews Road was the place where the 'Fever Cart' was kept. Anybody with diptheria or scarlet fever used to have to go away to the fever hospitals on the Welford Road. They had a special cart with windows in, which you couldn't see through. Also, they used to have to take the bed and the bed linen to be (fumigated). When they had a house that was infested with lice they used to take the beds and treat them in this place too. It was horse drawn. Belonged to the Borough.

Home Dentistry

Eileen Allard: (Speaking about Jim) That day he went out and had a drink. he had a tooth what was loose and it bothered him. So he got the kids what was round the green. "Come on," he said, "If you want to see something." He took them up the loft. Took an old fashioned iron with him and a lump of string. He threw that over the beam in the loft and tied the other (end) on his tooth. He let the iron go and out came the tooth. All the kids went running down the stairs out there. They hadn't seen anything like it.

Jim Allard: That's how I used to take my teeth out.

EA: Oh, they were running down the stairs! Three at a time!

JA: I said, "There's the tooth then." They said "Ooh!"

EA: Quick, run and tell their mother.

The Slipper Baths

The café on the corner of St. Andrews Road and Spencer Bridge Road – currently known as 'Super Sausage' – was originally built to have 'slipper baths' for the neighbouring area.

Pat Edwards: I can remember going and having baths 'cause none of the houses had bathrooms. It was sort of cubicles with baths in. A lady attendant used to run the bath water and tell you when to go in. You took your own soap and towel.

Jim Edwards: In the men's side, he'd know how long you'd been in. If he thought you'd been in too long he'd bang on the door, "Come on, it's about time you was out of there!"

PE: You couldn't fill the bath yourself. The lady had to put the bathwater in so you had a certain amount of water. You couldn't put any more hot water in, so if you stayed in too long the water would get cold.

JE: Had the cold tap used to run? I can't remember. But they had a tap which fitted into the top and turned the water on. He filled (your bath) up and that was your ration. It was always a good amount.

There was a waiting room, both the men's and the women's. In there was a ticket office, where you paid for your bath, and you could buy a tablet of soap or a bath cube. I believe you could hire a towel. So it was an 'all-in' service. All day Saturday there was a queue. Especially Saturday afternoons because people worked Saturday morning those days. And you sat round in the queue like in a barber's shop. Anywhere like that, there was a queue Saturdays.

PE: The (slipper baths) went on right up until the '50's. 'Til most of the flats were built.

JE: 'Til getting on for 1960 when they started pulling down Bath Street and Scarletwell Street. (It) was taken over straight away as a café and has been ever since.

Sunday Schools

Josephine Kent: We used to have to go to Sunday School three times on a Sunday. I went down Doddridge in Castle Street. You went in the morning and they gave you a little yellow ticket with a number on and then, perhaps another week it was an orange ticket. Then you had to go back in the afternoon and you went back again in the evening.

Julia Bush: What was the ticket for?

JK: Well, you took that home to prove that you'd been.

Irene Swainsbury: We used to go to Sunday School down Horsemarket.

JK: The little chapel on the corner of Horsemarket Gardens.

IS: That's right. I can always remember that I had a friend and we used to meet and go in. They used to have certain Sundays (when) everybody used to have to take eggs. This friend of mine, she'd got a brand new hat – 'cause we had to wear hats – and my brother and I stood behind. His egg broke and it went all over her hat. She stood in chapel crying because she'd got to go home and tell her Mum she'd got egg all down her hat. And my brother was frightened because he hadn't got his egg to give up to the vicar. He'd broke it!

St. Andrews Church

Mary Smith: Dad was a big churchgoer. He was a churchwarden at St. Andrews church.

Kate Wills: So, Sunday, you were up for, what, the first service of the morning?

MS: Yes, we used to go at 11 o'clock. I was in the choir. Then, in the afternoon, it was half past two – Sunday School – 'til about half past three. Then we'd go to the half past six service at night. Very often we used to go to 8 o'clock communion, Christmas Day.

I remember the old church. I can see it now. It's a shame they ever knocked that down. Behind the altar there was the Lord's Prayer in one panel. There was the Creed in another and I forget what. It was a lovely old church. They'd got a lovely organ. They'd only got one bell there. There wasn't a peal. I can't think of the name of the man who rang the bell, but he'd only got one arm.

Scarletwell Street Mission

Joyce Hall: My Father was in charge of Scarletwell Street Mission. That was attached to St. Katherine's Church. If they had got a vicar at the church then my Father was very often asked to go down to Scarletwell Street and take the services there. Mainly in the evenings. I think they only had a Sunday evening service. If we'd got an interregnum at church and my Father was needed to take the service at St. Katherine's, then they would put another lay reader in for Scarletwell Street. My Father took duty quite a lot at St. Katherine's Church, because those days we used to have quite long interregnums when there wasn't a vicar. He was superintendant of the Sunday School and, really, church warden. He did the lot. In those days they didn't have the staff.

I went a lot with him (to Scarletwell Street). It was a little Mission church, one floor of a building with a little vestry at the back. He used to just come in and take the service for the people in that area. They would just like to drift in. (It was) almost evangelical, you sang sort of and clapped to allelujahs. It was a sort of simplified service to accommodate people that like a more free and easy way. There was no choir.

The Church of England were sensible enough to have these little Missions. My Father used to put his cassock and surplice on. The people just drifted in, had the hymns and the prayers and the little five minute talk. That's all they needed.

They were always the same ones. (There) were people that used to help. One would come in and put a bowl of flowers there. One would give the books out. One would put the hymn numbers up. And Lil and her Mother used to wash the table linen for the altar. They kept the vestments beautifully white and they cleaned – it was only a wooden floor with a few pews in. It was something in their lives and they were always terribly reliable. If there were 50 there, it was always the same 50. My Father would stand at the door and have a little word with them all as they went out. That was people from Scarletwell Street, Bath Street, Little Cross Street, not much further than that. It was just the little community that used the place.

The End of St. Katherines

Joyce Hall: Kings Heath was the first area to rehouse the centre of town, so all the people were moving out to Kings Heath. They wouldn't come back to St. Katherine's Church. I can remember when it was full of people in my Father's day. I have pictures of the choir, 20 or 30 strong.

My Father and the church wardens fought. I can remember them having meetings because he was so sad that the church was going to be pulled down. It broke his heart. They fought and fought. But they said, "All your congregation's gone." All that was left was Gold Street with all the shops and College Street and the Drapery. That was our parish, as it were. There was no one then who would have supported St. Katherine's Church. So, of course, it was pulled down and it was turned into St. Katherine's memorial square.

We were amalgamated to All Saints, the town church, that is All Saints with St. Katherines even now. A lot of people went to St. Andrews Church along St. Andrews Street, which has again been pulled down. Some went to St. Sepulchres, there are still St. Katherine's people there. So they split up and went to different churches around the area. But that was the end of an era.

Sports

John Stevens: There used to be football played, rugby football, in that area of the town. There used to be a team based at the Green Dragon on the Mayorhold called St. Georges. They used to have a good cry G-E-O-R-G-E-S – Georges. Then there was a public house in Scarletwell Street just below the Mission Hall, named the Friendly Arms, they used to have a rugby team there. There were rugby teams at all the factories over that area of town. My Father's three brothers, two brothers played for St. Georges, one brother played for the Progressives, and they each of them won medals with the Lewis Shield. And then I followed on and I won it... We played on a Saturday afternoon.

Kate Wills: Where did you go to play?

JS: There used to be a pitch on Victoria Park. Victoria Park was run through by a stream which runs into the Nene. On the other side of the stream, beyond the bowling greens, there used to be a rugby pitch which ran down to Gandy's Bakery. That's gone now. There used to be a team that always played on Dallington Park. On the Racecourse there was always a rugby pitch.

Ron Johnson: Did you play cricket right through the year?

Ron Draper: No, mostly it would be a summer game, because in the winter we used to have football. We used to go and get a little red ball off old mother Trasler on the Mayorhold – only about 4-5 inches in diameter. We'd have a whip round or take a few empty bottles back and get thruppence. Play football on there (the Orchard), use the shed at one end as one goal 'cause it had three or four posts holding the roof up, then we used to draw a goal on the other end 'cause it was a wall. We could even play at nights sometimes because they used to have a gas lamp in there.

RJ: Did the Boroughs boys used to go and watch the Cobblers or the town cricket?

RD: Well, you'd spend days up there in the school holidays. Go up there with the old jam sandwiches and your bottle of kali water.

Alf Humphrey: When there was a football match down the meadow – where the car park is now – we always had a gang to play Scarletwell Street. (It) was always a big rivalry. We used to play Sunday afternoons, very near kill ourselves. We used to play football for a penny.

Richard Foreman: The team that won had the penny?

AH: It wasn't a team, a gang. There might have been twenty one side and twenty the other. Kick each other to death for this here penny. We'd all put a penny each before we started. If there were twenty one side and about twenty the other, there was forty pence in the kitty, so you had (tuppence) back, you see. We didn't play for an hour and a half then. We started about two o'clock and perhaps carried on 'til six. Oh, it was murder them days.

Then we decided to form a football team. So we went along and asked the neighbours if they'd give us a few odd coppers for kit and then we had some little raffles and all that. Then we got our kit and bought the goal posts. We used to have to put the goal posts in somebody's back yard. Every Saturday morning we used to carry the goal posts from here to Cow Meadow – Beckett's Park now. We didn't have to pay for pitches then, the first ones that got the posts up on the pitch could have it for the Saturday afternoon. We nearly always had that pitch, the slope as you go down towards the river.

RF: So what time of the morning would you have to get there?

AH: Before seven o'clock. They were proper hour and a half games, you know. A referee and everything - not like we was down the meadow.

We played for two or three years like that and then we gradually went to join Grafton YMCA.

RF: So you got incorporated into it. When you were playing with the Compton Street team, who would you have games with.

AH: You could always get a game every Saturday.

RF: Was it from all over town?

AH: All over the town you see. The chap that was Secretary, he'd get in contact with different teams and it was always well known for matches.

RF: Would people come to watch?

AH: Oh yes. Eventually I finished up playing for one or two teams. I played for Adelaide longest – they used to play on the Racecourse. We used to have crowds to watch them. It was called the Adelaide but we used to strip out at the 'Horse and Jockey' pub. We was in the league then. I finished up with Kingsthorpe – they played up Knight's Lane – and then I broke my ankle and I packed up altogether. A lot of the pubs that time of day, ran teams themselves. The 'Shakespeare' down Marefair – that was a good team.

Compton Street Football Club, 1917.

Albert Hassall – Compton Street Football Club – how it got started:

Imagine a crowd of youngsters with a ball that they made themselves. It consisted of plenty of paper, made into a ball, covered in sacking and tied very tight. We then used to go to the meadow, that was the waste ground at the back of the Four Fishes Cafe (now the Super Sausage). It is now a car park.

A ball made of paper didn't last long, so we got together and decided we would form a team. But we had a problem. We had no money and our parents could not spare any. Then someone had an idea.

At that time there was a public house on the corner of every street. We asked them if they would help us and they said they would. Mrs. Buswell, who owned a grocery shop in Compton Street, told us she would buy the football to start us off. We sent away for some scented cards and got our parents to sell them in the pubs.

I can still smell the scent now. Some of them were terrible. I think every house in the street smelled of scent.

We also contacted a carpenter in Harding Terrace, who said he would make the goal posts for us cheap.

So, with the money we and our parents collected, we bought the shirts and socks. Compton Football Team was formed.

Grafton Street YMCA

Peter Verrechia: I can go back to the YMCA on Grafton Square. Used to have a bath Sunday night, Friday nights. Only the lads you know. Used to belong to it. Used to fight to get in first to get all the hot water. Used to get a penny bath. Warm bath. Take your turn. That was in Grafton Boys Club.

Ron Draper: It was a Church Army Captain ran it when I used to go there – I can't remember his name. As I say, I was only 8 or 9. Later as I got older, I went to the Stute, the YMCA institute along Grafton Square. We used to call it the Stute.

Ron Johnson: What did you get up to down there?

RD: Everything! Gym, snooker, ping-pong, and there was a little tuck shop. Lovely little boys club.

Lucy Starmer: This man reckoned the YMCA building was the Duke of Grafton's town house, because (the) stonework round the windows was so good (and) how well it was built. He reckons that's why it was Grafton Street, because of the connection.

As a small child I remember word got round: "The Duke of Grafton's coming." We used to run to the door on Grafton Square. The carriage would come up and the servants would get the old Duke out and put him in an old-fashioned bath chair, like they had along the sea front, and wheel him into the institute.

There was a butchers shop underneath and then people lived at the side of it. Well I reckon, Miss Newsham ran this club. Then she started a Scout Troop.

Grafton YMCA Boys' Club, 1968

A Boroughs Wedding

Richard Foreman: You got married in 1933, can you tell us about your Wedding?

Elizabeth Whitney: Yes. I was married on Regent Square Chapel. We didn't have a reception like everyone else. My husband made the wedding cake and somebody across the road got us some barrels of beer. They were in the parlour. And then, of course, we'd got about 50 people coming to tea. In a little two-roomed house!

RF: This was your parents' house?

EW: Yes, and a lady over the road cleaned at the Chapel in Spring Lane and she said we could have the tea in here as long as we didn't have any drink. So we had it set out in the... well, my husband being a baker, the butchers shop was next door to the bakery and they cooked us a whole leg of pork. Well, when it was cooked, he didn't think it smelt as good as it might, so they sold that in the Co-op shop (laughter) and cooked us another one. But we had a good do, I mean, I had a white wedding and my uncle, Uncle Alf, he was in charge of the beer and he was drunk before anybody else started (laughter).

Pat Edwards: Where was the beer then?

EW: In our Mother's front room, and Uncle Alf was in charge of the beer...

PE: So everybody had their tea and then came over to the house?

EW: No, they were drinking the beer before. And I went to Birmingham on my honeymoon so I didn't know what happened after. After the wedding and we had our tea, we went off on the train to Birmingham.

RF: Did most people in the area have the same kind of wedding?

EW: The same kind of wedding. I mean that was a good wedding really. But you couldn't afford a big (one), not like they do now.

The End of the Boroughs

Richard Foreman: Did the way of life change in the Boroughs after the First World War?

Lucy Starmer: They began to pull the houses down, the side of our Post Office, about '36. Well, that was only three years before the war started. They moved them to Kingsthorpe. Well then, the communities broke up. You see, they didn't know what each other was doing. It was because they moved them from the old haunts into the new. That's what happened.

RF: How did people react to that?

LS: Well, they just kept saying 'Never see anyone now'.

Kate Wills: Were they pleased to be going?

LS: Well, they didn't make any trouble about it. Some of the houses were getting...

KW: Dilapidated. And they were going to better appointed premises.

LS: Well, yes. You see, and they'd have flush toilets and so forth. And a bath you see. Because I never had a bath until I moved to my flat in 1960.

Joyce Hall: It was a gradual process. When I started moving away, they were beginning to do a lot of rebuiding. The slum clearance began after the war – I think that's when the change in the town started. So, by that time, the young people and the children that were living opposite us were all moving away. Parents were dying or else they were transferred over to Kings Heath which was the first area for rehousing the slums. Then, soon after that, they began to pull down the houses opposite us.

The one person we were very friendly with, immediately opposite, was the lady who used to come in and help my mother with a bit of cleaning. She was very sad. She sort of said, "Oh, this is the end of our association." She moved away and we kept in touch with her, but soon after she was ill and died. One or two died quickly then, as and when their houses were being knocked down. I think (it was) the shock of thinking they were going to move. You found there was a sudden deterioration of everyone. They'd stayed in their little homes and managed. As soon as there was an upheaval, it did something to them. It broke them down. You felt they were giving in and thinking, well, they didn't want to move away. This had been their life. Quite a few of them died quite quickly.

Up the street I can remember there was a bottling firm, a Mr. Howard, who used to be the main producers of bottles of pop and fizz and that sort of thing. He was going to move away and couldn't take his business. This was another thing. When they were destroying or getting rid of the slums, in those days, you couldn't take your businesses anywhere else. You were absolutely stuck because there were restrictions – you couldn't take a yard with trucks and horse shoeing equipment into a residential area. So they knew they'd got to leave it all behind. You couldn't ever put that sort of business anywhere else, because it was sort of natural. Where (our) trucks sat was plain earth, it wasn't a paved area. It was a sort of natural building. At the side were the stables where the horse used to be tethered. You couldn't really build that anywhere else.

Within ten years of the war, the whole of the area had been altered completely. It had all gone. There's nothing left except a little bit of Horsemarket and Scarletwell Street.